The Nontraditional Learner's Guide to Success

Creating an Informal Support Network

R. Lee Viar IV, PhD

authorHOUSE®

AuthorHouse™
1663 Liberty Drive
Bloomington, IN 47403
www.authorhouse.com
Phone: 1-800-839-8640

© 2011 R. Lee Viar IV, PhD. All rights reserved.

No part of this book may be reproduced, stored in a retrieval system, or transmitted by any means without the written permission of the author.

First published by AuthorHouse   09/27/2011

ISBN: 978-1-4567-6228-5 (sc)
ISBN: 978-1-4567-6229-2 (ebk)
ISBN: 978-1-4567-6230-8 (hc)

Library of Congress Control Number: 2011907932

Printed in the United States of America

Any people depicted in stock imagery provided by Thinkstock are models, and such images are being used for illustrative purposes only. Certain stock imagery © Thinkstock.

This book is printed on acid-free paper.

Because of the dynamic nature of the Internet, any web addresses or links contained in this book may have changed since publication and may no longer be valid. The views expressed in this work are solely those of the author and do not necessarily reflect the views of the publisher, and the publisher hereby disclaims any responsibility for them.

I thank God for all the strength and blessings that he has bestowed upon me to have given me the opportunity to reach this point in my life and to be able to share what I believe will help others. Without Him nothing would be possible. This book is dedicated to my family who was, and continues to be, a true inspiration to me in all of my endeavors. The chain of love as I call it begins at the top with my grandparents; the late M. Loraine and George P. Rung Sr., my aunts and uncles, Walter L. and the late Andrea Rung, the late Diane R. Mickle, Therese R. and Wolf Kutter, Angela L. Rung, George P. and Lee Ann Rung Jr., Edward J. Rung, Monica R. and Donald Murray, Joseph M. Rung, and Alesia R. and Paul Carey, and of course, my loving and long supportive parents; Roy L. and Elizabeth R. Viar III. The source of my motivation and energy is my children: Alexis, Robertson, Ashley, Loraine, and Justin, the true lights of my life. And my source of love and laughter, my soul mate and best friend, my wife, Lori, the living embodiment of "behind every good man is a good woman" is verified in her. Thank you all and God Bless!

Contents

Preface x

Acknowledgments xiv

About the Author xvi

Chapter 1 - Challenges of a Nontraditional Learner 1

    Experiences 4

Chapter 2 - Educational Situation 8

    Questions Asked of the Nontraditional Learners 10

    Glossary of Terms 13

    The Participants and the Process 16

Chapter 3 - Is This Really Me? 18

    Bowen Family Systems Theory 20

    The Olson Circumplex Model 21

Chapter 4 - Research Participants 40

    Participant Profiles 41

    The Presence of an Informal Support Network 42

    How the Presence of the Informal Support Network Impacted the Women 43

    How the Presence of the Informal Support Network Impacted the Men 43

    Impact of Support from a Husband/Wife Perspective 44

Chapter 5 - Themes and Sub-themes 50

    Theme 1: Participants Experienced their Informal Support Network As Having an Expandable Boundary 51

    Theme 2: Participants Experienced Their Informal Support Network As Varying in Strength and Influence 58

    Theme 3: Participants Experienced Their Informal Support Network as Having the Capacity to Magnify the Qualities for Success They Already Possessed 68

    Theme 4: Participants Experienced Their Informal Support Network as Having the Ability to Expand Their Capacity to Meet the Many Challenges Faced 71

    Theme 5: Participants Experienced Their Informal Support Network as an Evolutionary Process Throughout the Educational Journey 76

Chapter 6 - Conclusion or…Just the Beginning? 78

Nontraditional Learner Reference Guide 81
Summary 83
References 85
Author Index 95

Preface

"Let us think of education as a means of developing our greatest abilities, because in each of us there is a private hope and dream which, fulfilled, can be translated into benefit for everyone and greater strength for our nation."

~John F. Kennedy

This book investigates the influence of an informal support network on the growing population of nontraditional learners and explores the implications of this support network for learner persistence and success. Obviously, the end objective is success for the nontraditional learner. Success can be defined in many different ways and can mean a multitude of different things to each individual. This success can manifest itself in the form of an intrinsic motivational purpose, for career advancement or continuing education. Whatever the reason, education is a precious gift and degree attainment should be encouraged, regardless of the learner's stage of life.

Who should read this book? Nontraditional learners, instructors of nontraditional learners, the support networks, and the nontraditional learners' mentors, as well as, counselors who are working with adult learners, will benefit from the insights provided herein. In addition, it is my sincerest hope that this book can act as a guide to assist working adult learners who enter institutions of advanced learning later in life to achieve their goal of earning a degree.

What's inside of this book? The first chapter of this book establishes a theoretical foundation based on an examination of current trends in education in general. The experiences of the nontraditional learner, both positive and negative, are introduced. The chapter concludes with a discussion of challenges facing the nontraditional learner as they pursue their college education. The context for the book is established in this chapter.

In Chapter Two the current education situation is examined, more specifically, the enrollment and graduation rate of nontraditional learners in higher education. Later in the chapter, I introduce the research methodology that was used and the type of information that was gleaned from my study. A list of questions that eventually became the framework for my study is also discussed. Lastly, a glossary of terms is provided to avoid any confusion with the context of the terms used throughout the text.

Chapters Three and Four focus on the nontraditional learner and the participants of the study. Chapter Three identifies some of the characteristics of the nontraditional learner. A nontraditional learner reading this book can conduct a mini-assessment to determine if they have similar characteristics. Although the experiences of the nontraditional learners presented within this book vary in relation to the types of support received, situations surrounding their experiences, and the informal support networks themselves are commonly shared among other nontraditional learners. Chapter Three helps to highlight some of these commonalities so that the nontraditional learner reading this book can identify with the experience and determine what they need to do to succeed, and whether they will be successful in their educational journey.

Chapter Four provides a more in-depth profile of the nontraditional learners who shared their experiences with me during the writing of this book. Later in this chapter, the presence of an informal support network is established. In addition, the impact of the presence of an informal support network on both the male and female nontraditional learners is discussed. An analysis of the themes and subthemes that were uncovered in my discussion with the nontraditional learners is provided. The chapter closes with an in-depth look at each of the individual themes as they relate to the experiences of each learner.

In Chapter Five, the results of my research, interviews, and personal experiences are compiled to establish the significance of the study. I conclude in Chapter Six by creating recommendations to help the nontraditional learner to be able to develop the characteristics needed to succeed and overcome the challenges that they will face as they pursue their education.

Acknowledgments

The author wishes to acknowledge the people and organizations whose information was invaluable and provided the inspiration to keep writing.

To Dr. John Creswell, for his time and guidance in assisting me to complete the research for this endeavor. To Dr. Gordon Graham, a very special thank you, a student could not ask for a more supportive and motivational mentor than this wonderful man. Drs. Victor Klimoski and David Balch; without whose help, insight, and professional guidance, this would not have been possible. Also, Reverend Michael Jendrek, Father Mike who has been a dear friend and spiritual advisor throughout some wonderful and difficult times.

To the nontraditional learners who dedicated their time and shared their experiences so that others may be successful in their educational endeavors and without whose contributions this manuscript would never have been completed.

To the Association of Nontraditional Students in Higher Education and U.S. Department of Education for providing valuable research and reliable information that helped to support my work.

To all of my instructors throughout my academic journey whom I was able to gain invaluable knowledge and understanding that enabled me to reach this point.

I would also like to thank the external reviewers who gave their time and expertise in providing invaluable feedback in previous drafts. Thank you all and God Bless!

About the Author

Dr. R. Lee Viar IV earned a PhD in Post-Secondary Adult Education and Training, MBA, and is currently pursuing a second PhD in Organization and Management. He is a Certified Postsecondary Instructor and published author with over ten years of university teaching experience at both undergraduate and graduate levels. As an adjunct professor, he instructs approximately sixty-six online courses each year at various universities, including traditional universities that offer online courses. He is affiliated with the graduate program in business specializing in management and marketing as well as adult education specializing in online instruction. He has won a number of awards for his contributions to the classroom as well as the continued success of his students. He also works as a marketing consultant, has served on a number of dissertation committees, and has served on faculty development and assessment panels as well as a Lead Business Faculty. In addition, he is also a course developer for the business and education curriculums, and has been named as an Honorary Board Member of the MERLOT Business Editorial Board. He lives in Maryland with his beautiful wife and five wonderful children and continues to write.

Chapter 1

Challenges of a Nontraditional Learner

"Life's challenges are not supposed to paralyze you; they're supposed to help you discover who you are."

-Bernice Johnson Reagon

"The graying of America has had a powerful impact on all segments of American society including businesses, government, health care, and education" (Craig, 1997). However, what obstacles, if any, does the nontraditional student experience in the educational genre and how can the informal support network help to overcome these obstacles? The impetus of this book was my desire to help as many students as possible regardless of age to succeed in college. Adult students form one of the most rapidly growing segments of today's college student population. According to The Chronicle of Higher Education Almanac (1999), adult students make up approximately 63% of the student population. In a study conducted by Bendixon-Noe, the nontraditional student makes up 45 percent of all undergraduate students enrolled in higher education and the numbers are increasing each year.

What prompted you to decide to return to the college environment or attend college for the first time? In order to truly appreciate this situation, let's first establish some history and develop a foundation for this book. This influx of older or mature students has been prompted by demographic, economic, and technological changes and developments. In addition, the older population is living longer, retiring at a later age, and enjoying a healthier lifestyle more than ever. Therefore, the need or desire to further either their personal, career, or educational goals can now be fulfilled. This was previously not an option in the form of credit or noncredit college-level courses. However, just as traditional students must face obstacles in their educational journey, so do the older population. "Adult students often must confront issues of balancing family and career demands" compounded by the "restrictions on their study time due to domestic commitments" (Richardson & King, 2002). The two major commitments for an adult are their family and career. A third commitment consisting of the rigors and demands of attempting to obtain an education can be stressing to the individual. Juggling a family, career, and any educational endeavor means more demands on time and less of this precious commodity to deal out.

The college industry as a whole has realized the growth potential of the nontraditional student population and to some extent has addressed and made adjustments to help accommodate this segment of the student body. When the number of college-age cohorts dropped dramatically in the late 1970's and into the 1980's, many schools turned to adult education as the means to support the college or university and also to draw on this growing market segment. This strategy provided even more impetus to potential nontraditional learners to continue their desired educational journey.

According to the United States Department of Education, National Center for Education Statistics (2003), nontraditional learners can be classified into several categories based upon characteristics known to adversely affect the persistence and the attainment of their degrees. The more adverse characteristics that each learner possesses determine the appropriate risk factor assigned to each learner. For example, a traditional student has no risk factors, a minimally nontraditional student has one risk factor, a moderately nontraditional student has two or three risk factors, and a highly nontraditional student has four or more risk factors. The term, student, used throughout this book refers to the "nontraditional learner" if he or she met one or more of following characteristics: delaying enrollment in college after graduation from high school, being a part-time student, working at least 35 hours per week, and being financially independent. Within the context of this book and based upon the research, other considerations included whether the nontraditional learner was married or had children.

"Nontraditional students are much more likely than traditional students to leave postsecondary education without a degree". This startling statement, sad as it may be, comes from the United States Department of Education (National Center for Education Statistics, 2002). What is the contributing factor to this staggering fact about adult learners who do not or cannot realize their educational goals? Examining some of the various factors that can contribute to this statistic will provide a better understanding of the statement and determine its validity. Self-reflection is very important at this point. Look at your own life, be very candid, and ask yourself, how would I assess my factors?

Adult students confront some unique problems in adjusting to a traditional academic setting. They express fears about competing and fitting in with 18-22-year-old students. This is especially true in these ever-growing technologically advanced times when the typical nontraditional learner may feel either intimidation from the technology or fear of not being able to learn the technology necessary to succeed. Although these adult learners may be effective problem solvers because of their many challenges in life, adult learners may exhibit fewer skills for coping in an academic environment (Richardson & King, 2002). In a study conducted by Bird and Morgan, it was found that, "Failure to anticipate at least some of these changes, and most importantly to involve the family and gain informed support for this transition, may create family discord and impair one's ability to proceed with study" (2003). In another study conducted by Bauman, Wang, DeLeon, Kafentzis, Zavala-Lopez and Lindsey (2005) the following insights were established:

Indeed, the importance of family and social support to the success of nontraditional students have been underscored across several research studies, with at least three unique aspects of social support being identified: (a) instrumental support including practical kinds of help or tangible aid, such as financial assistance, that is provided by family and friends; (b) informational support consisting of information and advice that help an individual cope with personal problems; and (c) appraisal support including praise and validation that bolster an individual's self-evaluation.

More than 60% of the participants in the study reported they received strong support from friends and family members (Bauman, et. al., 2005). Is this a leading indicator of success for the nontraditional learner that remains to be seen? Unfortunately, the mere presence of an informal support network can have either a positive or negative effect on the returning nontraditional learner. It is then the responsibility of the adult learner to adapt to the level of support they are receiving in order to be successful and obtain the desired outcome, a college education. It is important to keep in mind that the nontraditional learner needs to be able to accurately identify the level and type of support being offered by the informal support network. If it is positive, the nontraditional learner needs to have the ability to nurture this environment. At the same time, the nontraditional learner needs to be able to distance themselves from unconstructiveness and negative influences as much as possible. It is important to be mindful of the fact that the support networks and the corresponding influence can and will impact you. However, the nature of the impact and its affect will depend on you alone.

Experiences

My experiences, both personal and professional, which have been almost an odyssey taking nearly two and a half decades to fully develop, were the primary reasons for writing this book. Education can be considered a key to success in the work environment. In many instances, experience is not as important as a degree specifying completion of a certain curriculum when it comes to workplace success. I experienced this firsthand when I became a displaced worker even though I had over seven years of experience but lacked a degree.

My educational journey may not be the textbook example of how to obtain a degree. Upon graduation from high school, I attended a local junior college and earned an Associate's degree, while working full-time at a local bank. This financial institution based compensation and promotions upon job performance and only partially considered the level of education for the individual employee. I had progressed up the ranks in the financial institution from a bank teller, collection agent, loan interviewer, to finally a mortgage and personal loan officer. However, after over seven years with the bank, the financial institution and career that I had worked and strived so hard at was bought by a holding company and the loan department was eliminated in deference to the existing loan processing center over two hundred miles away. Continuing my education was not in my immediate plans at that time. Therefore, I then went to work for another company for eight years until I became tired of training individuals for positions that I was qualified for but could not be assigned to because I did not meet the formal education requirements. As a consequence, I became a nontraditional learner and reenrolled in college. In reference to a support system, my enrollment counselor at the time questioned if I could make it. He plainly stated that he doubted that I would successfully complete my degree since I had a family and financial obligations not including the pending financial debt for my college education. He stated my time away from the classroom and work obligations would be too great to overcome. Talk about a negative influence. After all, this was a question that I had already pondered myself, and having been asked this question by the counselor only added to my apprehension.

Through a series of career related occurrences and experiences, I found myself needing to continue my education. At the age of thirty-four with three children, going back to college was not high on my list of goals, not to mention the fact that when I was younger, my academic achievements and experiences were not necessarily fond memories. I had struggled with certain courses and came to the conclusion that if I struggled with them in my late teens and early twenties, I would definitely struggle with them at this stage of my life. Reestablishing my study habits, learning how to take tests again, and working on projects were challenging enough without the added financial burden of tuition and lost income. Even more important was the loss of family time. Nevertheless, a Bachelor of Science Degree in Business Administration and subsequently a MBA in Management and Marketing were seen as an avenue to a better career and future. Consequently, my own journey led me down a path with some twists and turns, but I was always filled with support from my various family members. Yet I wondered, after hearing stories from my fellow adult nontraditional learners of conflict, jealousy, and even marital problems, was my story unique, or was I being naïve thinking everyone had the support that I enjoyed. My deep interest in this topic was the impetus for undertaking this book and my own journey to examine my own lived-experiences and assumptions.

During the initial phase of my return to education, the unceasing informal support demonstrated by my now five children, Lori my wife, and parents assisted, motivated, and kept me on the path to success, even during my lowest points when I neared the point of even considering dropping out all together. The attainment of my MBA was at times a struggle, yet the support did not wane, it was there when it was needed and in the background when it wasn't required. Subsequently, upon arriving at the decision that a Doctorate Degree in Education would be the best thing for my career, not to mention the lifelong dream of mine to earn a PhD, which I thought would always remain just that, a dream, I embarked on my doctoral journey. My family, starting with of course God, my grandparents, my parents, aunts and uncles, my loving and supportive wife, and my children have all nurtured and engendered an atmosphere of internal motivation. This support network had sustained me even when it felt as though the journey was pushing me to the limits of my own endurance.

With this experience acting as a foundation, it further raised my interest and curiosity in this subject matter. Therefore, I began to conduct some qualitative research into this area for part of my doctoral studies and hence, subsequent post-doctoral research. The topic of my inquiry had been established and evolved into the informal support network and the nontraditional learner. The premise had always remained the same, were my experiences commonplace or a personal phenomenon? Was my journey unique or was it typical among returning adult students in the college environment? Did the presence of an informal support network have a significant influence on educational success or did it merely generate a pseudo feeling of satisfaction and accomplishment?

What could be gleaned from the experiences of others who fell under the growing category of nontraditional adult learners?

Chapter 2

Educational Situation

"Results show an increase in the enrollment of nontraditional learners, yet graduation completion rates do not correspond."

-U.S. Department of Education

This brings us to our current educational situation. The number of nontraditional students has steadily increased, and statistics are demonstrating that this population, in general, may experience considerably more psychological and social difficulties than traditional students (Leonard, 2002). Statistically, "results shows an increase in the enrollment of nontraditional learners, yet graduation completion rates do not correspond" according to the U.S. Department of Education (National Center for Education Statistics, 2002). Furthermore, "the graduation rate is lower than traditional students and this study can offer some insight into the contributing factors of this situation." Even though these statistics are somewhat disturbing, the purpose of this book is to ensure that you or your loved one doesn't become one of these statistics.

College enrollment in higher education for students over the age of

25 has increased 114% since 1970; whereas enrollment of traditional-age students has only increased 15%. Educators, counselors, mentors, families, and learners will benefit from the additional research into this rapidly changing segment of the student population (Clinton, n.d.). Not only will this book serve as a guide to better assist you in your educational journey by providing you, the nontraditional learner, with a framework to identify those in your support network that will be the most valuable to you in this endeavor, it will also help you to determine the nature of support you will need in order to succeed. Most importantly, your informal support network, which is imperative to your success, will gain the knowledge and strategies to help you effectively capitalize on both your intrinsic and extrinsic motivators in order to succeed.

Throughout my research into this area, I have adopted a research methodology based upon the premise of a qualitative study. According to Dr. John Creswell, whom I had both the privilege and pleasure to meet and speak with, a qualitative study is:

> An inquiry process of understanding based on distinct methodological traditions of inquiry that explore a social or human problem. While conducting a qualitative research project, the researcher builds a complex holistic picture, analyzes words, reports detailed views of informants, and conducts the study in a natural setting (Creswell, 1998, p. 15).

With this as my selected configuration, I chose to utilize a semi-structured interview format when speaking to my research participants. This was a preferred method because it provided a wealth of information and insight from the participants' experiences. I was seeking to learn about the informal support networks from their points of view; consequently, the structure and format of the questioning and interview style were pliable. A phenomenological research design quickly lent itself as the most effective and efficient technique to be able to accomplish my goals. As a result, by having these nontraditional learners recall their own experiences through a series of in-depth interviews, I was able to gain important insight that I considered significant enough to be able to assist future nontraditional learners, educators, administrators, and the informal support networks themselves. What is my purpose for reviewing my methodology and how I accomplished this? The reason is simple, I want you the reader to be able to understand how I was able to bring together this information from other nontraditional learners and understand its significance.

Questions Asked of the Nontraditional Learners

Now, I had to determine what to ask the nontraditional learners who participated, and determine what questions would provide me with the answer to my question of, how this would benefit future nontraditional learners and their informal support networks. When I set out to develop specific questions to ask these nontraditional learners I realized quickly the importance of establishing the tone and framework of what I was attempting to achieve. It was imperative that I learn the meaning of the lived experiences of nontraditional learners embedded in informal support networks as they continue their educational journeys. To do that, I needed to find out whether the essential structure of an informal support network was unique or common in the success for the nontraditional learners. It sounds rather simple and straightforward; however, it probably took the better part of a legal pad to settle on this core question. Finally, with the primary question established, I then progressed on to set the more focused questions that I wanted to pose to my nontraditional learners.

The following questions became the framework for my nontraditional learners.

1. How does the informal support network contribute to the lived experiences of the nontraditional learner as you attend an institution of higher learning?

2. How does the informal support network detract from the lived experience of the nontraditional learner as you attend an institution of higher learning?

3. How does the informal support network contribute to the academic success of the nontraditional learner as you attend an institution of higher learning?

4. How does the informal support network detract from the academic success of the nontraditional learner as you attend an institution of higher learning?

5. What elements of the informal support network influence whether it is adding to or detracting from the lived experience and academic success of the nontraditional learner as you attend an institution of higher learning?

6. How did the various forms of informal support networks provided to the nontraditional learner impact you as you attend an institution of higher learning?

7. How did the various forms of informal support networks received by the nontraditional learner impact you as you attend an institution of higher learning?

I do not have any grandiose ideas nor am I presuming to have discovered the end all to be all in miracle solutions for how the nontraditional learner can be successful and therefore obtain their education and complete their degree program. Rather, it is my sincerest hope to be able to contribute to the existing body of knowledge regarding the success or failure of the nontraditional learner. However, I hope you can learn from these nontraditional learners' experiences. The relevance of this book truly emanates from my research participants themselves. It was the results of years of trials and tribulations of my research participants and their recollections of their informal support networks that truly contributed to my modicum of success.

Who is this book truly written for? The insights gleaned from my research and investigation will hopefully enable nontraditional learners, either entering college for the first time or returning to the college environment, to draw on the experiences of other successful nontraditional learners, including me, and to become more aware of the success factors or challenges that may assist or inhibit them. In addition, the new or returning nontraditional learners could benefit from this knowledge, capitalizing on the opportunity to determine if the various levels and types of support will be conducive to their individual needs. This book can also provide some useful insights that the nontraditional students will need to make their own assessment as to whether they possess the informal support network needed to aid in the successful completion of their education.

One of the key components of any informal support network is the family. This book can enable families of nontraditional learners to discover how they can best support the learning process of the nontraditional learner. The benefit of this knowledge can enable the families to be prepared to make a conscious decision on whether they will be willing and able to provide the necessary level and type of support the nontraditional learner truly needs. The type of support will vary from one learner to another depending upon their personal situations and circumstances. Obviously, established lines of communication will need to be present in order for this process to be of benefit. The nontraditional learner is going to need to adequately communicate to their informal support network what kind of support they require while at the same time, the informal support network will need to convey the type of support that they will be able to supply as well. One key point needs to be mentioned, the nontraditional learner needs to be aware that the support could and in some cases should manifest itself in the form of constructive criticism. The maturity level of the nontraditional learner needs to be in place in order to truly benefit from this mode of support and not merely take it personally as an affront to their work or method of learning. Again, this can be significantly easier said than done, but is it crucial for the success of the nontraditional learner. They have to be willing to learn from the typical sources of knowledge, for example, instructors, research, and textbooks, and also, from their informal support network and their feedback. This book can also benefit the advisors of nontraditional learners. The advisor has the ability to recognize and potentially influence the path of success for the nontraditional learner from the outset of their educational journey versus merely signing the student up for classes. More important, if properly trained, the academic advisors can identify possible issues or roadblocks for the nontraditional learner and take a proactive position and assist the learner. "A counselor who is inquiring about a student's social support network should recognize the role of the student as a member of a family" (Bauman, Wang, DeLeon, Kafentzis, Zavala-Lopez, & Lindsey, 2005). Again, referring back to an experience I had with my academic counselor, his negative influence could have had a grave impact on my decision to pursue a degree, rather, I viewed it as a challenge that come hell or high water, I was going to succeed, in spite of his opinion of my abilities.

Another segment that could potentially benefit from the results of my research and investigation is the faculty instructing nontraditional learners. Knowing the circumstances and situations facing the nontraditional learner in advance can better prepare the faculty member to be able to identify strengths and weaknesses of the nontraditional learners, therefore, allowing the instructors themselves to better assist them in the educational process. Many times, seasoned or veteran instructors can lose touch or forget what it was like to be an adult returning to the classroom after years or possibly decades, and its affiliated challenges and issues.

Glossary of Terms

Many scholars and educators have attempted to define the term nontraditional learner. Throughout this book you will come across key terms that may have multiple meanings. Although many of the terms can be easily dissected to find their true meaning, others may require some knowledge of alternative meanings when applying them to the type of research and scenarios presented in this book. In my efforts to develop a clearly defined explanation of what a nontraditional learner is, I developed a list of key terms and provide definitions that are workable for me that will hopefully also benefit the reader. The content and references in this book are reflected in these terms.

Bracketing describes the act of suspending one's beliefs about the reality of the natural world in order to study the essential structures of the world (VanManen, 2000).

Cohort A group of individuals who have a statistical factor in common; for example, year of birth (U.S. Department of Education, National Center for Education Statistics, 2000).

Enrollment The total number of students registered in a given school unit at a given time, generally in the fall of a year (U.S. Department of Education, National Center for Education Statistics, 2000).

Full-time enrollment The number of students enrolled in higher education courses with total credit load equal to at least 75 percent of the normal full-time course load (U.S. Department of Education, National Center for Education Statistics, 2000).

Full-time-equivalent (FTE) enrollment For institutions of higher education, enrollment of full-time students, plus the full-time equivalent of part-time students as reported by institutions (U.S. Department of Education, National Center for Education Statistics, 2000).

Graduate An individual who has received formal recognition for the successful completion of a prescribed program of studies (U.S. Department of Education, National Center for Education Statistics, 2000).

Graduate enrollment The number of students who hold the bachelor's or first-professional degree, or the equivalent, and who are working toward a master's or doctor's degree. First-professional students are counted separately. These enrollment data represent those students who are registered at a particular time during the fall. At some institutions, graduate enrollment also includes students who are in post baccalaureate classes but not in degree programs (U.S. Department of Education, National Center for Education Statistics, 2003).

Informal support network Students benefit from the efforts of both professional educators and those individuals who offer their assistance in various forms. For the purposes of this study the informal support network consists of those individuals who offer substantial help to the student but who are not one of the professional educators working with the student.

Interdependent Mutually dependent (The American Heritage Dictionary (2000).

Locus of control the source to which one attributes power to control the rewards of one's life (Pilisuk, Montgomery, Parks, and Acredolo, 1993).

Nontraditional learner For the purposes of this study a nontraditional learner has been defined as a student who has any of the following characteristics (a) delayed enrollment (does not enter postsecondary education in the same calendar year that he or she finished high school), (b) attends part time for at least part of the academic year, (c) works full time (35 hours or more per week) while enrolled, (d) is considered financially independent for purposes of determining eligibility for financial aid, (e) has dependents other than a spouse (usually children, but sometimes others), (f) is a single parent (either not married or married but separated and has dependents), (g) does not have a high school diploma (completed high school with a GED or other high school completion certificate or did not finish high school) (U.S. Department of Education, National Center for Education Statistics, 2002), or (h) is older than 24 years of age.

Part-time enrollment The number of students enrolled in higher education courses with a total credit load of less than 75 percent of the normal full-time credit load (U.S. Department of Education, National Center for Education Statistics, 2000).

Personal Network group of people who are in relationship with an individual and are committed to helping that individual attain his or her dreams and life goals (FIF, n.d.)

Post baccalaureate enrollment The number of graduate and first-professional students working toward advanced degrees and students enrolled in graduate-level classes but not enrolled in degree programs (U.S. Department of Education, National Center for Education Statistics, 2003).

Systems Theory the transdisciplinary study of the abstract organization of phenomena, independent of their substance, type, or spatial or temporal scale of existence. It investigates both the principles common to all complex entities, and the (usually mathematical) models which can be used to describe them (Heylighen, 1992).

The Participants and the Process

I had the privilege of interviewing eleven nontraditional learners for this book. The nontraditional learners were comprised of both men and women ranging between 33 and 67 years of age. All of my learners were considered to be nontraditional learners and were either still in the midst of their educational journey or had recently graduated within the last three years. The participants were pursuing Bachelor's, Master's, or Ph.D. degrees in a variety of fields and disciplines. After spending numerous hours with each research participant either in person or on the telephone, it was assumed that adequate trust and rapport had been established in order to gain significant and in-depth responses during the subsequent interviews. In addition, it was understood that the responses and opinions expressed by the learners accurately reflected their circumstances and meaningfully relayed their experiences. They were also given ample time to reflect on the topic of discussion before the interview and were therefore able to mentally assemble as much of their thoughts and recollection as possible. From my standpoint, it was also assumed that I was able to effectively bracket my own experiences and perceptions while collecting the information needed for my research. Bracketing, also referred to as reduction, describes the act of suspending one's beliefs about the reality of the natural world in order to study the essential structures of the world (VanManen, 2000). In addition, VanManen states, "the aim of the reduction is to reachieve a direct and primitive contact with the world as we experience it rather than as we conceptualize it". This was important to accomplish because my objective was not to merely relay experiences from my own educational journey, which I did, but rather to gain the insight of other's experiences and how these nontraditional learners were successful, thereby hopefully providing the necessary information for others to be successful as well. By truly gaining knowledge of how others have succeeded on their educational journey while facing a host of challenges, you will have the opportunity to see where others failed and avoid those pitfalls and have the opportunity to make your educational journey a more pleasant experience instead of one that is perhaps difficult and prompts you to quit. Quitting or stepping away from your education for a period of time should be your absolute last resort. The following data helps to further illustrate this point. "At a time when college degrees are valuable--with employers paying a premium for college graduates--fewer than 60 percent of new students graduated from four-year colleges within six years" (Carey, Hess, Kelly, & Schneider, 2009).

Chapter 3

Is This Really Me?

In order to truly be able to gauge your need or level of support you may require or the level of support you may offer a loved one or friend, it is important to be able to identify these common characteristics of the support format. In addition to these common characteristics, it is important to familiarize yourself with the trends and patterns regarding growth in the enrollment of nontraditional learners in postsecondary educational institutions.

To understand the influence of the informal support network on the nontraditional learner, consider the family the student is embedded in, since its members often make up a significant portion of the network. The family unit as an entity has been defined in various ways. What its function and role are in the evolution of individuals has been debated for years and will continue to be because individual families and even the institution of the family itself is constantly growing and evolving. There are several preconceived notions and beliefs about nontraditional learners and informal networks that include family members that need to be addressed. A study conducted by Moen and Sweet (2004) found that the ramifications of the outdated conception of the family and the workforce are compounded by a secondary belief in the standardized, lock-step life course that, for workers, is patterned after traditional male career paths. The first step was to be earning an education, followed by full-time employment and finally by full-time retirement. At the university level, most schooling is still designed for the young student without job responsibilities; even though 40 percent of students enrolled in colleges or universities are ages 25 or older. As well, growing numbers of both men and women are returning to school in order to shift careers or to continue educational or career goals that have been interrupted by the demands of caring for children (Moen & Sweet, 2004). In addition, Moen and Sweet found that these nontraditional learners "face serious challenges managing the complexities of their work and family lives". The informal support network, particularly those aspects of it composed of family members, can make the nontraditional learner's journey both easier and more complex. Either way it will have a significant influence on the learner's education and is worthy of careful investigation. Close personal relationships are the main resource from which social support is derived (Pilisuk, Montgomery, Parks & Acredolo, 2002). Furthermore, this study by Pugliesi and Shook, found that social support resources are influenced by personal, social, and environmental factors. In addition, "the sum total of one's personal ties, the informal network, is a critical social resource utilized in efforts to cope with various life stresses and problems". Information, practical assistance, and socioemotional support may all be derived, at least in part, from informal networks. Thus, the characteristics of informal networks affect the probability of the receipt of social support. Returning to school is often a stressful situation filled with anxiety and doubt about whether it will be a successful journey. For the nontraditional learner, this stress is often compounded with career obligations, family responsibilities, and challenging financial commitments. However, the informal support network can be a resource for the student. It can assist in offsetting the numerous distractions and obstacles that could and do impede the academic journey of the student.

Students do need access to information and resources; they also need personal support provided by formal and informal social networks. So, why is the informal support network so important? Thompson, Jahn, Kopelman and Prottas (Thompson, Jahn, Kopelman, & Prottas, 2005) describe the informal support network as a "conceptually meaningful construct that can be assessed by individuals and aggregated across individuals, in a manner akin to psychological climate." They also find that "perceived organizational family support is comprised of two dimensions of support: (a) tangible support, which taps perceptions of instrumental and informational support, and (b) intangible support, which taps perceptions of emotional support". It was further asserted that, "in the situation of the nontraditional learner, in most cases, organizational family support refers to intangible support, such as emotional support". However, some instances of support from the informal support network take the form of tangible support, such as proofreading college work or consulting on ideas relating to the subject matter. The value or importance of the assistance in a positive manner cannot and should not ever be underestimated or discounted. The sense of pride and accomplishment can act as a phenomenal positive motivational tool for the nontraditional learner as well as motivating the informal support network by merely reviewing a research project or essay and providing constructive feedback in conjunction with a, job well done, and keep up the good work. Now that is support that each and every one of us can feed off of and utilize.

Bowen Family Systems Theory

A different point of view regarding the importance of the family system dynamic is the Bowen Family Systems Theory. Within the framework of this theory, the family is viewed as an emotional unit and the theory draws on systems thinking to describe the complex interactions in the family unit (Bowen, 2004). Bowen also found that it is the nature of a family that its members are intensely connected emotionally. Consequently, family members can have a profound effect on other family member's thoughts, feelings, and actions so much that the impression of living under the same emotional skin can exist. Bowen's theory substantiates the idea that the informal support network can have either a positive or negative effect on the learner. Furthermore, the support system has the potential to influence nontraditional learners by facilitating or hindering their education. Dr. Bowen points out that people solicit each other's attention, approval, and support and react to each other's needs, expectations, and distress. The connectedness and reactivity make the functioning of family members and other support network members interdependent; however, the networks differ in the degree of interdependence. If nontraditional learners feel an interdependent connection with their network, they may solicit their families for the attention, approval and support needed to continue on with their education. If an interdependent connection of adequate strength is not being felt, the family members may be offering the attention, approval, and support but the nontraditional learners may not be receptive to it or to the forms in which it is being offered. Again, this goes back to the point that the nontraditional learner needs to be receptive to the informal support being provided.

The Olson Circumplex Model

The Olson Circumplex Model can help illustrate why the informal support network has such a significant influence on nontraditional learners. Olson's model is based on systems theory. "A systems theory proposes that objects in the world are interrelated to one another" (Seepersad, 2002). Olson developed his model in terms of three main dimensions: family cohesion, flexibility, and communication. Family Cohesion is defined as "the emotional bonding that family members have toward one another". This emotional bonding can be viewed as the want or desire for the family members to be successful and given the opportunities to achieve their goals. Olson also states, "family flexibility is the amount of change in its leadership, role relationships, and relationship rules". Family flexibility reflects the changing stages of the family unit as the members of the family unit age and have their roles changed or even reversed. A typical role reversal takes place when grown children become the caregivers of their elderly parents. According to Olson, "family communication is measured by focusing on the family as a group with regards to their listening skills, speaking skills, self-disclosure, clarity, continuity-tracking, and respect and regard". In the context of this book and situation, communication within the support network is particularly important when it comes to accurately identifying the request for and coordination of assistance to the nontraditional learner.

The informal support network's potential to have a lasting effect on the nontraditional learner is often influenced by the learner's previous experiences. For example, in a study completed by Richardson and King, research found that "many adolescents failed to continue their formal education after the minimum school-leaving age" (Richardson & King, 2002). Richardson and King's study concludes that the negative experiences within the learners' families or at school often disrupt their subsequent attempts to realize their intellectual potential by returning to formal education as adults. Their research adds important insight. "Paradoxically, if these adults are to be successful in negotiating their entry into higher education, then compensating for and, to some extent, overcoming these disadvantages may become strengths for them as learners". Negative experiences from the past can be converted into positive motivation for nontraditional learners. It is this type of attitude that needs to be adopted.

Bird and Morgan (2003) conducted a research study on mature-aged learners. Some interesting points of view and experiences were exposed in their research. For instance, the impact that study has on family life is one of the more difficult issues for the prospective distance education learner and their families. The issue regarding the time commitments of the studying process for the learner could very easily be applied to the conventional brick and mortar classroom setting. It was also found that "recognizing the additional financial burden and decreased availability for family life due to study commitments, most adult learners need the support of their partners or loved ones. Although partners may be supportive in principle, the full impact of this transaction has yet to be understood or experienced" (p. 9).

The results of Bird and Morgan's study support some of the concepts introduced in this book; primarily the need to include the family in the learning process as a whole. The informal support network is strengthened if children of the nontraditional learners are included in the process of helping the learner succeed. There is the additional benefit of enabling nontraditional learners to positively influence their children by demonstrating the value of an education, which may ultimately encourage them to pursue their own education. Also, the required time commitment not only affects the learners and their partners, but also the children of the learners. If the nontraditional learner can involve the children in the learning process, the time justification can be more palatable for all parties concerned. The process of negotiation with family members can occur prior to commencing the educational journey. However, Bird and Morgan also stated "prospective students also need to know what assistance they can access if they find themselves under considerable stress" (Bird & Morgan, 2003, p. 9).

It cannot be assumed that an informal support network will be a positive and constant presence. "I always need to remind myself that support can be both positive and negative and support has an associated intensity," Oehlkers (1998). Oehlkers further states:

> We probably all have come to realize that persistence by the adult learner in an educational program may have more to do with support received by family and friends than the quality of the program. And yes, negative support by the family may in some cases because the learner to persist to affect the changes the learner seeks (p. 1).

For those nontraditional learners considering the online educational option, Greer (1998) found that the most common success factors identified by learners were time management, being self-motivated to attend class, having appropriate technology tools, and having supportive friends and family since Web-based courses require such a large time commitment. One of the conclusions from Greer's study was that the amount of time, commitment, and dedication needed for online learning is equally high to that needed for traditional classrooms and requires the same informal support network. Greer substantiates this by saying, "support is needed from all areas: family, friends, co-workers, and other web students," (p. 7).

Schopler and Galinsky (2002) offer an explanation for the proliferation of informal support networks over the last two decades.

> Support groups serve a useful function in helping people deal with stresses related to common crises, life transactions, and chronic conditions. In addition, their proliferation over the past two decades is associated with the increasing need for formal and informal sources of support in the wake of rapid social change, geographic dispersion of families

and friends and cutbacks in funding for human services. (p. 195)

Schopler and Galinsky (2002) went on to define support groups as forms of "social networks that have the potential for bridging gaps in service and for providing emotional support, guidance, and information" (p. 195). However, because references to support groups have become widespread, confusion has arisen over how these groups that provide emotional support, guidance and information differ from other groups such as mutual help groups, self-help groups, and treatment groups, which provide support that is initiated by professionals and frequently are affiliated with a national or regional sponsoring organization. As well, the term "support groups" according to Schopler and Galinsky, generally implies the coming together of individuals with some pressing common concern who are willing to contribute personal experiences and engage in the development of a cohesive, supportive system. The informal support network can enter into a partnership with the learner that will aid in the educational process, or it can interfere with the process by acting as a demotivational and disruptive factor. This concept needs to be examined and embraced by the nontraditional learner.

A series of studies conducted by Schuller, Preston, Hammond, Brassett-Grundy, and Bynner in 2004 regarding the influences on the adult learner found that "education is a significant mediator of social, economic and demographic influences which produce life-course changes, and is a marker for the establishment of families" (p. 81). They went on to state, "returning to the world of learning as an adult may not necessarily be considered "normal" and the transition may not necessarily be an easy one". They also state, "family members can provide the impetus for an individual to engage in learning, but they, or the presence of a family unit, can also be a hindrance" (p. 92). Many of the observed experiences from the nontraditional learners in this book were positive in nature and contributed to academic success for the student. However, many experiences were not as productive and made it more difficult to achieve academic success with serious and long-lasting effects on the family unit as a whole. What does this mean to the future nontraditional learner?

The concept that the informal support network exists as a

strengthening force or an impediment is going to have an impact on the nontraditional learner's educational journey. Nontraditional learners may benefit by taking a proactive approach to identifying, reducing, or removing potential barriers to their educational endeavors. Or, the learner could capitalize on the strengths of the family support network, excel, and succeed in reaching his or her educational goals.

The influence that a family has on the nontraditional learner can be real or perceived. The learner's perception of lack of support can be generated by their own feelings of guilt for not being available for their spouses or children, in a sense, a self-imposed punishment for continuing his/her education. These perceptions can be fostered or totally displaced by the support network from the family. However, all of these feelings, emotions, and opinions can and do have major implications and ramifications upon the student. To further substantiate this assertion, research conducted by Benshoff and Lewis (1992) involving nontraditional learners finds seven developmental issues for women who return to school, two of which are, "feelings of responsibility for maintaining their role within the family" and "insufficient support from family for returning to school" (p. 2). However, the perception of "lack of support" is not relegated to solely female nontraditional learners.

In a study by Chao and Good in 2004, published in the *Journal of College Counseling*, nontraditional college learners were queried to learn what their perspective was of their college education. The participants' perceptions of pursuing college education resulted from dynamic interaction among several factors. Chao and Good found that "central to the interaction was a sense of hopefulness that participants held toward their decision, struggles, and perceptions about the future" (p. 7). One of the contributing factors to this hopefulness felt by the nontraditional learner was the student's support system. "Family, friends, and academic professors were crucial components" (p.7). Chao and Good's study also found that "nontraditional students' decisions to pursue more education affected their relationships with family, friends, and others. Their commitment to the student role motivated them to negotiate their work, family responsibility, and interpersonal relationships to achieve their goals in completing their college education" (p. 9).

The following paragraph included in Chao and Good's research describes the changing relationship one participant experienced after her return to school.

> My husband encouraged me to earn a college degree since he knew I was stuck with my work. Then we negotiated on sharing our responsibilities of taking care of kids. He sometimes needed to be at home when I was in school. But, you know, my kids liked to do their homework just like I was doing mine. So I guess I set up a role model for my kids (p. 9).

This is an obvious example of a positive, reinforcing experience for the nontraditional learner. Two key factors in this success story were communication and a bringing together of the family as a unit so that everyone would have an active role in the process.

Rendón (1998) touched on an interesting point regarding this issue. As a result of researching nontraditional learners, she came up with the term "validation." Rendón describes validation as being a time "when faculty, students, friends, parents, and spouses made an effort to acknowledge these students and what they were trying to achieve" (p. 3).

A personal network, similar to a social network, is a group of individuals that provides some form of guidance or encouragement. Timmons, Moloney, Dreilinger and Schuster, found that "a personal network is basically everyone that a person knows. This includes both formal and informal network members" (p. 2). As well, formal network members take a more professional role such as school counselors or teachers. Informal network members are people close to you, like your friends, family members, and others you may have met in social organizations, sports teams, religious organizations, or even in your neighborhood (Timmons, Moloney, Dreilinger & Schuster, 2002). They also believe that personal networks can guide the self-determined person as they solve problems and support them when important decisions are made. Also, people from the personal network help teach new skills as goals are achieved.

Despite the importance of family, the fact that many nontraditional learners are away from home can make the support network of friends and fellow students even more important (Groben, 1997). In addition, families are not feeling the pressures of finals and may not be able to completely understand these pressures. Groben finds that friends have their own stress to consider and may not be as supportive as the learner would like, but at the same time, they have a greater understanding of the stress level during finals week.

The nontraditional learners enrolled in colleges across the country face a myriad of obstacles. A study completed by Timarong, Temaungil, and Sukrad found that the obstacles facing adult learners today are making the transition to student even more challenging and difficult.

> **Barriers for adult learners may include inability to obtain financial aid and poor financial planning; lack of persistence or motivation; gender; age; language; lack of support from employers, friends, and family; socioeconomic status; educational background; intelligence; poor study skills; poor stress management; lack of counseling services; and lack of flexible class scheduling (n.d., p. 3).**

Furthermore, Seibert and Karr noted, "make your family and friends feel included, not excluded...the more they know about what you do, the more they will understand and support you" (2003, p. 115). They also stated, "family and friends need to know they are still the top priority in your life. Give them good quality time. Good personal relationships are an essential success foundation as you juggle work, home, and school" (p. 116).

A study concerning nontraditional graduates, (Simcox, 1998) examined the phenomenon of persistence and its link to the students' successful completion of a degree. This study described persistence as a multifaceted phenomenon encompassing physical and emotional attributes such as time, effort, energy, and the need for support of others. Family, peer, and faculty support and commitment were instrumental to the completion of the programs undertaken by the participants. Simcox concluded that school and related activities consumed most of the waking moments of the students, forcing a loss of connectedness with family and friends. However, by being persistent, the student was able to succeed, even with the loss or decreased presence of the family. DuBois (1998) found that "family played a large part in the student's persistence" (p. 48). In addition, "a few students were very much loners and had no support systems. For them, the desire to achieve something for themselves kept them going during the rough times in class," (p. 69). Another example of the effects of a negative family influence is found in an article by Kerka (1995), which points out that personal reasons such as family problems, lack of childcare, and job demands are often cited as the cause for withdrawal.

> As a member of an informal support network, a nontraditional learner needs to be willing to both receive and provide support. When receiving support from various sources, the adult learner should not be personally offended or take what is being said out of context. Rather, it should be viewed as constructive criticism from individuals, who are trying to contribute to the nontraditional learners' success and may have the significant talent, ability and knowledge. However, regardless of the learner's talent and knowledge, collaboration between the nontraditional learner and the support network will most likely lead to furthering the educational process. Kirschner and VanBruggen in 2004 stated, "to collaborate is to work jointly with others especially in an intellectual endeavor. Thus, the work that is to be carried out is learning, and the way that it is done is together with others" (p. 135). "Students need to trust each other, feel a sense of warmth and belonging, and feel close to each other before they will engage willfully in collaboration and recognize the collaboration as a valuable experience" (Rourke, 2001, p. 1).
>
> Forming a sense of community, where people feel they will be treated sympathetically by their peers, seems to be a necessary first step for collaborative learning. Without a feeling of community, people are on their own, likely to be anxious, defensive, and unwilling to take the risks involved in learning. (Wegerif, 1998, p. 48)

Field's research completed in 2005, confirms an existing hypothesis about the mutually beneficial relationship between social connectedness and lifelong learning.

> The highest level of positive attitudes towards an active

approach to learning were found among those who are actively engaged, whatever the activity; these are followed by those who are actively hostile; while those who are indifferent show the lowest levels of positive support for an active approach to learning (p. 7).

The same applies to the family and personal support network for an adult learner. The key question is, when and under what condition is this network utilized? An adult learner, unsure of when to seek support could use Timmons, Moloney, Dreilinger, and Schuster's ways to "reach out to your network." This tool can be of great benefit to anyone who is considering furthering his or her education.

1. Ask for help when you are facing big decisions in your life.

2. Take the time to tell people what you are thinking about, share your goals, and the challenges you may be encountering.

3. Be specific about the ways that you would like people to help.

4. Don't be afraid to ask more than once.

5. Realize that members in your network will play different roles and you will not get the same thing from each member.

6. Realize that network members aren't always able to help. There may be times when you ask for help and they are not able to give it to you.

7. Keep your network updated on your progress. People like to help and it will make them feel good to know that you are working toward your goals.

In order for a support network to be truly beneficial, the nontraditional learner must keep in communication with the members of their network. Otherwise, those network members will not know how to assist the learner or know if any assistance is needed.

In another study conducted by Sciba (n.d), the concept of the impact of the family support network, either in a positive or negative posture, is further solidified. Sciba finds that "nontraditional students, who work fewer hours and have older children, report less personal-emotional distress; however, reducing work hours or child-care responsibilities is not an option for many nontraditional students" (n.d., p. 4). In Ortiz's research, one respondent commented, "her spouse is very supportive-as long as he is not very affected!" Sciba also reports that "students with a social support network of family, friends, and coworkers report higher academic and personal-emotional adjustment. Some respondents in Ortiz's study stated that spouses and children were resentful of the amount of time devoted to college" (p. 4).

Donaldson (1999) examined the key elements that affect learning and stimulate adult's experiences in college. Individuals within the social setting of students, but not part of their classes were discovered to have a significant influence on the students' return to higher education. He noted varying levels of support provided by these support group members and saw that the support either enhanced or detracted from the psychological and value orientation components of nontraditional learners when they engaged in their collegiate experiences. This book contributes to the growing body of literature that illustrates the value or detriment of an informal support network for the nontraditional learner. Furthermore, it should be viewed as a further testament for the nontraditional learner to recognize and assess their individual situations.

A nontraditional learner, as defined by Benshoff and Lewis, is "an adult who returns to school full- or part-time while maintaining responsibilities such as employment, family, and other responsibilities of adult life" (1992, p. 1). In the same study by Benshoff and Lewis it is stated "adult students need help in building their self-confidence as students, in acquiring or refreshing study skills, and in managing their time and other resources while in school" (p. 2). Nontraditional students need many different kinds of support and assistance from family, friends, and institutions of higher learning. Further research suggests, "both sexes have difficulties juggling the roles of student, worker, and family member" (Muench, 1987, p. 10).

Rendón (1998), points out that the nontraditional learners he researched were excited about learning new things and making new friends; but they also spoke of loss. They talked about the emotional discomfort involved in separation from their family and friends. This sense of loss can be further compounded by the fear of failure having been out of the classroom environment for ten or twenty years. However, an informal support network can counterbalance the sense of loss and compounding fear of failure. According to Rendón, nontraditional students were more persistent when someone helped them believe that they were capable of doing academic work. This is further evidence of the value of an informal support network for the nontraditional student. "Members of the informal networks were generally ready to state their opinions and views and had no compunction about giving directive guidance" (Semple, Howieson, & Paris, 2002, p. 3). Fram and Bonvillian found full-time employees who are also part-time students describe themselves as highly stressed, always trading off between work, family, and school, often lacking sufficient sleep. Focus group interviews conducted by Fram and Bonvillian with nontraditional learners elicited this response; "I feel terrible when my three-year-old daughter cries for attention, and I have to leave her and go off to classes" (2002, p. 31). Another study conducted by Bell (2003) found that "nontraditional students face different hurdles in the classroom today. Unrealistic goals, social-familial problems, poor self-image and a sometimes excessively practical orientation are among the nontraditional students' problems" (p.159). In addition, nontraditional students have tensions not only in the classroom but outside the classroom as well. The level of stress experienced by nontraditional learners can be at times overwhelming; however, the informal support network can help the learners stay focused, and remind them of the purpose for their pursuing an education. This research found in this section was used to convey some of the challenges and circumstances that the nontraditional learner faces and to point out that these are not that unique. Many learners have experienced these challenges and circumstances and have endured, as you will in your educational endeavor.

    Lundberg (2004) points out that traditional and nontraditional learners share many commonalities as well as many differences.

Like younger students, their learning was enhanced by

peer learning and high-quality relationships with others on campus. However, unlike younger students, their learning was not hindered by working many hours off campus or commuting. Thus, the social arena remains important for adults when those social relationships are related to educational endeavors, but assumptions that adult students are inherently at a disadvantage because of their multiple obligations off campus is not supported by this study. Older students appear to have developed a way of managing such time limitations to nullify their effects in ways that their younger counterparts have not (p. 671).

Lundberg's study demonstrates that outside obligations are not necessarily a detriment to the nontraditional learner; they can be managed and capitalized upon. Keep in mind that the spirit of capitalizing on this journey can be filled with pride and a sense of accomplishment and that the informal support network can enhance your experience.

A report from the Department of Education entitled "Findings from the Condition of Education 2002, Nontraditional Undergraduates" describes a nontraditional learner as one who has any of the following characteristics: (a) delayed enrollment (does not enter postsecondary education in the same calendar year that he or she finished high school), (b) attends part time for at least part of the academic year, (c) works full time (35 hours or more per week) while enrolled, (d) is considered financially independent for purposes of determining eligibility for financial aid, (e) has dependents other than a spouse (usually children, but sometimes others), (f) is a single parent (either not married or married but separated and has dependents), or (g) does not have a high school diploma (completed high school with a GED or other high school completion certificate or did not finish high school).

The U.S. Department of Education (1998) developed an index of risk ranging from 0-7 that classifies the nontraditional student according to seven characteristics known to adversely affect persistence and attainment. A nontraditional learner can be characterized as minimally nontraditional (one risk factor), moderately nontraditional (2 or 3 risk factors), or highly nontraditional (4 or more risk factors). Some of the nontraditional learners interviewed for this book possessed each of the aforementioned attributes.

Persistence is a challenge for nontraditional learners. According to a recent study "among nontraditional students who enrolled in 1989-1990 with the intention of obtaining a bachelor's degree, only 31 percent had earned one by 1994, relative to 54 percent of their traditional counterparts" (Taniguchi & Kaufman, 2005, p. 912). Taniguchi and Kaufman's study further revealed that the most apparent reason part-time learners have a lower chance of obtaining a degree is that it takes them longer to progress from basic to more advanced courses. In addition, many studies have shown how the nontraditional learners' family environment can be both enabling and constraining for their academic endeavors. "Spouses may provide support by paying for college expenses and taking on a larger share of housework so that their student-spouses can focus more on studying" (Taniguchi & Kaufman, 2005, p. 916). This would require that obvious lines of communication be in place between the learner and the spouse/children to request this assistance, and more important, the noted benefits for both the learner and the family unit. This point should not be overlooked, while on your educational journey, why not enjoy it, but more important, why not allow your support network benefit from it and enjoy it as well?

According to John Field, a published author and professor of lifelong learning, the concept of social capital is generally used to refer to the resources that people derive from their relationships with others. In fact, Field defines social capital as consisting of "social networks, the reciprocities that arise from them and the value of these for achieving mutual goals" (Field, 2005, p. 1). Field comments that people can use their social capital to gain access to skills and knowledge in a variety of ways. Field utilizes Robert Putnam's work on social capital to further elaborate on his insights.

> Social capital is built particularly effectively through civic engagement, which appears to be more or less synonymous with active citizenship...active citizenship is an important source of social capital because it is the main way in which people, particularly those who are strangers to one another, experience reciprocity through their pursuit of

shared objectives. This in turn helps to create a dense web of networks underpinned by shared values and producing high levels of social trust, which in turn fosters further cooperation between people and reduce the chances of malfeasance. (p. 2)

Bauer and Mott (3) developed a detailed description of motivational factors associated with individuals between the ages of 25 to 35 years of age. They discovered that universally, the love of family and security were ranked with the highest priorities. Similarly, an empirical study by Chartrand (1992) examining the nontraditional learner's adjustment to the college environment found that "family and friends outside the school environment serve as primary sources of emotional support for the student" (p. 193). There were three sets of variables in Chartrand's study, the third of which, environmental variables, was most relevant to this book. These variables were described as the crucial antecedents of student retention for the nontraditional learner. Chartrand wrote, "finances, hours of employment, outside encouragement, family responsibilities, and the opportunity to transfer would influence academic and psychological outcome variables as well as the decision to drop out of school" (p. 193). Chartrand also found, "consistent with predictions of the results, family and friend support was positively and directly related to both the absence of psychological distress and intent to continue" (p. 201). Chartrand further stated, "previously, family responsibilities have been identified by nontraditional students as a source of stress and a reason for college withdrawal" (p. 203). However, in this same study it was discovered that family responsibilities did not meaningfully contribute to perceived psychological distress or to intentions to continue in school. What can be gleaned from this study? It shows that the family support and responsibilities are at different levels, but at any level, its influence upon the learner is significant, although the influence can be either positive or negative. However, it is important to remember that the absence of this informal support network does not mean that the nontraditional learner will not succeed.

There is evidence that the informal support network and locus of control are interlinked for the nontraditional learner. Locus of control has been associated with several aspects of social support. According to Pilisuk, Montgomery, Parks, and Acredolo in 1993, locus of control refers to the source to which one attributes power to control the rewards of one's life. Individuals with an external locus of control believe their rewards, or more exactly their reinforcements, are under the control of powerful others, luck, or fate. Those with an internal locus of control believe their reinforcements are contingent upon their own behavior, capacities, or attributes according to Pilisuk. This study found evidence that individuals with an external locus of control experience pain and distress as less manageable and more prolonged than individuals with an internal locus of control. One of the most significant statements from the Pilisuk et al. study in terms of its relevance to this current study is that, "control is, in turn, a reflection of the social network" (p. 149). Control in this incidence refers to the ability of the individual to respond to their duties, regardless of the set of duties, based upon the assumption of receiving adequate support from the family support network. According to Pilisuk et al. "one maintains control by meeting responsibilities to kin and friends and by receiving assistance from the network. (p. 150)" In addition, "confidence in one's capacity for control reflects security in the network - a knowledge that its presence will endure through periods of duress" (p. 149). If the nontraditional learner is meeting his or her responsibilities to the informal support network, as far as communication and nurturing the informal support network is concerned, he or she can enjoy a measure of confidence that the support will be returned.

"Since 1970, the enrollment in higher education of students over the age of 25 has increased 114%; whereas the enrollment of traditional-age students has only increased 15%" (Kemper & Kinnick, 1990, p. 535). Kempher and Kinnick further state, "the influx of nontraditional students indicates an increased access to older students through the front door of higher education" (p. 535).

Even though the enrollment statistics for nontraditional learners have increased and there is no viable reason to believe that this trend will not continue, there is one distressing trend to consider. Eppler, Carsen-Plentl and Harju's research completed in 2000, found that "older students are more prone to dropping out of school due to conflicting commitments, such as family and work, or because they perceive the college atmosphere as less supportive" (p. 356). Statistically, this makes sense, if enrollment is increasing for this particular age group, then the dropout rate can be expected to increase as well for this segment of the college population. But, are the grounds for this increase in dropout rates due to intrinsic or extrinsic reasons and motivational factors that can be addressed by the informal support network, or does it fall under the auspices of the college itself? Moreover, is it the responsibility of the nontraditional learner to request such support? Pride is a wonderful thing; however, at times it can present itself as an obstacle.

In an age of rapid economic and technological change, lifelong learning can provide benefits for individuals and for society as a whole according to the U.S. Department of Education in 2003. Studies conducted by the National Center for Education Statistics showed that in 2003 most lifelong learning activities were formal activities including basic skills training, apprenticeships, work-related courses, personal interest courses, English as a Second Language (ESL) classes, and college or university credential programs. According to the U.S. Department of Education, NCES report, the overall participation in adult education activities was 46.6 percent, up from 41.1 percent just six years previously in 1995. It is important to note that the nontraditional learners interviewed in this book have reached a minimum age of 25 years.

Presently, nontraditional learners make up approximately one half of all college students nationwide and this figure is expected to increase (70). One tip UCLA recommends for the nontraditional learner returning to the school environment is to find academic and emotional support through friends, classmates or a support group, and to involve their family in their schooling experience. The importance of enlisting the support of an informal support network prior to entry into the traditional classroom setting is crucial in increasing the chances of success for the nontraditional learner (UCLA WRC, n.d.).

The nontraditional student has finally begun to receive the attention of not only the college admission offices and student loan organizations, but also the United States Senate. On April 29, 2004, Mrs. Clinton of New York introduced a bill pertaining to the nontraditional learner to the Senate of the United States. One of the purposes of the bill was to provide higher education assistance for nontraditional learners. The bill makes possible both initial and continued financial support for the nontraditional learner in the form of grants and loans. The rational for providing this aid emerges from the obstacles faced by nontraditional learners such as family obligations and career commitments that are not usually faced by traditional students. The proposed title of the Act is the Nontraditional Student Success Act. As of this book's publication, this Act is still being debated and amended.

According to a U.S. Department of Education's report, entitled "Findings from the Condition of Education 2002, *Nontraditional Undergraduates*", traditional undergraduates are generally able to direct most of their energy toward their studies, while older students, parents (especially single parents), and students who work full time have family and work responsibilities competing with school for their time, energy, and financial resources. The report went on to state a total of 39 percent of all postsecondary students were 25 years or older in 1999 compared with 28 percent in 1970 (U.S. Department of Education, National Center for Education Statistics, 2002).

The nontraditional learner population is recognized as such a large percentage of the student enrollment that an association was formed. The Association for Nontraditional Students in Higher Education's (ANTSHE) purpose is "to be an international partnership of students, academic professionals, institutions, and organizations whose mission is to encourage and coordinate support, education, and advocacy for the adult learning community" (Association for Nontraditional Students in Higher Education, n.d., p. 1). There has been an annual nationwide celebration of nontraditional learners scheduled each November for the past several years. Its goal is to foster recognition of nontraditional learners for their accomplishments and to improve their learning environments. Participating in organizations such as this not only provides avenues of support, but also offers networking opportunities.

Deciding to go back to college is exciting and challenging, but it is also stressful. In 2002, Wilson found that even those learners with adequate finances, personal confidence and high self-efficacy still identified family backing and emotional support as primary ingredients to success. She found that an important preliminary activity before returning to school was to "prepare the home environment, family, friends, and associates for the lifestyle adjustments" (p. 1). Wilson encourages family members and those close to the nontraditional learner to have a sense of shared ownership in supporting the college bound individual. Shared ownership could be developed through shared responsibilities. Examples of this include assisting in duties or chores around the house, having the older children or partner watch the younger children in an effort to give the learner time to do their schoolwork, or giving feedback and advice on assignments. These kinds of activities can heighten the level of involvement from the family and lessen the obstacles presented by the family. In addition, the support network can be further enhanced and everyone involved experiences a sense of accomplishment and purpose.

There are many types of networks: social, personal, professional, business, and family. According to Casey (2005), the goal and structure of a social network is, "connecting families to networks of friends, neighbors, kin, community organizations, role models, mentors, faith-based institutions, and other positive social relationships that encourage and provide neighbor-to-neighbor support and mutual aid and make people feel less isolated and alone" (p. 1). The research in this section further substantiates how this kind of effect is especially important for the nontraditional learner returning to school.

During the assembling of this book, the importance of an informal family support network in the educational process for the nontraditional learner in a positive or negative manner was investigated. The meaning of the term "support" in this context can be defined as, motivational, emotional, and psychological support for the nontraditional learner. The word "support" is not intended to include monetary assistance. Economic conditions and situations that are distracting and consume energy were not examined. During the research for this book, experiences of nontraditional learners as they interacted with their informal support networks were captured, codified, and analyzed to again, learn from those that have enjoyed success in and out of the classroom.

Selecting the right candidates to be interviewed required the process to be exact. The essential criteria for selecting learners required that they experienced the phenomenon being studied and shared my interest in understanding its nature and meanings. The learners selected needed to have the characteristics of a nontraditional learner, and needed to have experienced an informal support network in order to be considered, whether this support was considered to be positive or negative.

A phenomenological study is not without emotion. Dr. John Creswell, one of the most noted and respected qualitative research experts is quoted to have said, "The very nature of the qualitative study format generates stories and experiences that are emotional, close to the people, and practical" (Creswell, 1998, p. 141). Although some of the narratives relayed to me were filled with emotional content, I worked to sustain an impartial posture during the data gathering process, regardless of prior personal experiences. An unbiased account of the learners' thoughts and feelings is discussed later in the book in order for you, the reader, to benefit from not only my experiences, but from the experiences of the men and women who were kind enough to participate in my interviews and share their stories with me.

Once the data was collected in accordance with the best practices of conducting a phenomenological study, my analysis began. "The qualitative analyst's effort at uncovering patterns, themes, and categories is a creative process that requires making carefully considered judgments about what is really significant and meaningful in the data" Patton, 1990, p. 406).

The purpose behind citing all of these research reports and studies is to show you that some of the challenges that you may be facing in your educational journey or could possibly face are not uncommon and you are not alone. Your situation is not unique and hopefully, you can learn from the fact that others before you have faced some of the same obstacles and others will follow who will face them as well. However, that does not mean that history is destined to repeat itself with you. That is the purpose of this book, to arm you with the knowledge of how to attempt to avoid the pitfalls that have entangled others. Earning your degree is challenging enough, if available, why not utilize your informal support network for not only your own well-being, but to make everyone involved feel like they are part of your educational journey and celebrate your accomplishments.

Chapter 4

Research Participants

Before discussing what I had learned about the learners, I would like to provide you with a little background on each of them. It may be of some interest to examine these research participants to see if there are similar variables or characteristics that you may possess. First, there was a certain set of criteria that the learners had to meet in order to be considered eligible. The eleven learners were either current nontraditional learners in the midst of obtaining a degree or met the other specified characteristics of nontraditional learners. The pool of volunteers was assembled with the assistance of former colleagues, co-workers, and other acquaintances. Written permission from the prospective learners was obtained prior to their interviews. The learners reside in Maryland, North Carolina, Pennsylvania, Virginia, and West Virginia.

The interviews lasted approximately three to four hours in total for the initial interviews and subsequent follow up sessions; however, the interviews continued as long as relevant data was being provided by the learners. The venue where the interviews took place was typically relaxed environments chosen by the participants, where interruptions could be kept to a minimum.

At the onset of the interview, basic demographic information was collected from each of the participants, including their age, level of education attained to date, their educational discipline, years it took or will take to continue to pursue their education, and the format for the educational platform. These demographic questions served the double purpose of providing a warm-up opportunity for the interviewees and as a creation of a profile of the research participants. This information was provided so you, the reader, can see how you relate to the circumstances of the learners.

Throughout the next few chapters you will be able to relate even further with the learners by reading their direct quotes that further support the themes because "embedded quotes provide specific concrete evidence in the informants words to support a theme" stated one of the leading authorities in qualitative research, Dr. John Creswell (1998, p. 171). Pseudonyms were used in order to maintain confidentiality and the anonymity of both the participants and their families.

The purpose of the research found in this book was to describe the academic success and challenges of eleven successful nontraditional learners who had an informal support network. The central question establishing the framework for this book, what is the meaning of the lived experiences of nontraditional learners embedded in informal support networks as they continue their educational journeys?

Participant Profiles

A profile of the learners helped establish the credibility of their lived experiences and their qualification as nontraditional learners. Six of the eleven participants were men and five were women all ranging in ages from 33 to 67 years of age. Of the eleven learners, two men and one woman had successfully obtained their desired degree, including one PhD and two Master's degrees. The remaining learners were still in the process of obtaining their targeted degrees, which included bachelor's degrees in business and education, master's degrees in business, education, and psychology, and a doctorate degree in educational leadership. Eight learners were still active in the educational process, five were pursuing their degrees in traditional classroom settings and the remaining three were pursuing their degrees in online environments. The time and distance required to reach their respective college campuses ranged from fifteen minutes to one hour and twenty minutes each way. The three learners who had successfully completed their degrees took a combination of online and traditional classroom based courses.

Of the men, four were married with children, one was married without any children and one was single with one child. Of the women, two were married with children, one was widowed with children, and two were single with children.

All of the learners were employed for a minimum of ten years or were on active duty in the military, either stationed in the United States or overseas on a military base. Of the eleven learners, eight stated that they were working in their chosen educational/career field. Three hoped to advance to their chosen career field upon completion of their respective degrees.

The impact of financial obligations on the learners was also explored. One man and one woman funded their education themselves without the assistance of student loans or tuition reimbursement from their employers. The remaining nine received financial assistance through student loans or tuition reimbursement offered by their employers with the stipulation that they remained with their employer for a specified period of time after completing their degree.

The learners had lived through experiences associated with the phenomenon discussed in this book, not just as nontraditional learners, but also as individuals who took advantage of expanding their education regardless of the obstacles or barriers they faced. They were husbands, wives, parents, supervisors, professionals, therapists, lawyers, soldiers, and most importantly, they were students. They were students who combined family and careers with full or part-time programs of study in order to achieve their educational objectives and dreams.

The Presence of an Informal Support Network

In order to determine the impact that the informal support network had on the learners, it was important to first establish the presence of an informal support network. All five women stated that an informal support network existed. They described the individuals who formed their informal support network as family members, friends, and coworkers. The men stated that an informal support network existed as well. They also included family members among their supporters, but they defined friends specifically as lifelong friends, and co-workers as colleagues. They also added two additional categories: personal mentors and God. Obviously, these categories are not exclusive and you could have other unique categories.

How the Presence of the Informal Support Network Impacted the Women

Although each of the women stated that an informal support network was present, their opinions of the impact of their support network varied. Four of the women believed that if an informal support network had not been present in their educational journey, they would not have been able to complete their program and earn a degree.

> My fiancé and children are a great support system for me. They are the ones that provide me with the motivation and encouragement that I need to stay focused and keep going. Without them, I do not feel that I would be able to continue on with my education. (Lisa)

> If my husband hadn't been as supportive as he was, I wouldn't have done it and I wouldn't have been able to successfully complete my graduate degree. (Sarah)

However, when the fifth woman was asked the same question, she had a very different response.

> Yes, even if I had no support whatsoever, I would have still persevered; it would however have been significantly more challenging and difficult, but I truly believe that I would have been able to complete my degree on my own, I am my own person. (Melissa)

How the Presence of the Informal Support Network Impacted the Men

The men all acknowledged the presence of an informal support network. However, in contrast to the majority of the women, all six men indicated that even without the presence of an informal support network, it would have been possible or will be possible for them to successfully complete their educational endeavors.

I think it would not have been impossible to complete, but it would have been very difficult for me to do this if I had not had the support of my wife, family, and friends. Without their love and support, I am merely a shell, but they give me purpose and drive. Yes, I could have made it on my own, but I really would not have enjoyed it or would have been able to revel in the success with the ones who made it possible. (Charles)

> I would have been just as successful. My wife encouraging me was probably what had the most impact but I think I would still have had the same level of success. She has always been like the icing on the cake, but I truly believe that I could have done it on my own. (Keith)

> I think that I probably would have had some problems, but I still would have finished it. Whether or not I would have been as successful at it or completed it in the amount of time that I did, it's hard to say, but the positive support was there and that was helpful. Who is really going to say that if things were different, or if one thing or another would happen, I am just thankful that I didn't have to find out. (Daniel)

Is the apparent disparity of the opinions of the male and female research participants significant in regards to their presence of the perceived informal support network noteworthy, that will have to be left to your own discretion? Place yourself in the situation and assess your position and learn from these research participants.

Impact of Support from a Husband/Wife Perspective

The level of support and the manner in which it was given to the learners by their spouses and significant others varied greatly among the learners. The nature of this support and how it manifested itself was diverse while at the same time it was perceived as an emotional bond or barrier depending upon the type of support received. The importance of spousal support was discussed with eleven learners who were or had been married. The amount of spousal support varied and the results of that feedback included both current and former spouses. Of the participants who had former spouses, some received encouragement and others received opposition from their estranged husband/wife. Many of the learners who had a spouse at the time of the interviews emphatically stated that while support from their network was great, the support they received from their spouse, either positive or negative, had a higher level of impact. A number of learners described support from their spouses as including encouragement, assuming household work/chores, spending more time with the children, or providing quiet time in order to complete their studies. Learners also commented that support they received from their spouse or significant others also manifested itself in other forms. This was consistent for both the men and the women research participants.

> The encouragement I received was not only in the form of verbal prompting, but it also took the form of a shoulder to lean on or periodically to cry on, which meant the world to me. This is kind of hard to admit, being a retired Marine Corp. Sergeant, but we all need that extra hug or kick in the butt now and then to know that we are not in this by ourselves and for that, I will be eternally grateful to my ex-wife. (Daniel)

Another learner fondly recounted how his educational journey became a family journey filled with hard work and love.

> My wife really took a lot of pressure off of me by making a game around the house of which one of the kids could help Daddy the most this weekend. I really think it helped to bring us all closer together as a family and it brought me an instant cheerleading section of five kids. I think the two younger ones didn't understand, but the three older girls really take an interest in what I am doing. My wife has made a lot of sacrifices in order for me to continue on with

my education, I only hope that I will be able to return this massive favor someday to her. (Mark).

Another learner conveyed a touching story while fighting back tears as she recalled a very difficult time in her life.

> My husband believed in me when it felt like the whole world was grinding their heels into me, telling me that I was a failure and that I was stupid. I believed it until one day when I came home and found a textbook and a schedule of when we were starting our class together. He already had his Masters in English, but he was taking an Associates course with me. By enrolling me, I had no choice but to go, even though I knew I couldn't do it. But this wonderful man didn't give me any answers, but what he gave me were hints on how to study, a sounding board for my ideas, and a learning partner to grow with. Harold has been gone for over twelve years now, but I know that he would be proud of me because I went from having no degree to now starting my Ph.D. (Sarah)

The concepts of owing and repaying someone else became powerful motivators for the learners. They came to realize that they also needed to succeed in their educational endeavors because it would help them repay their family for their support with a higher level of income, a longer and more meaningful career, and an enhanced family identity and prestige. The more support the learners received the more they felt pressured by a sense of obligation that needed to be repaid to their families. They became increasingly motivated to repay this debt by succeeding in what had become a collective push by the whole family for success. However, could this sense of responsibility and owing create a new set of pressures to succeed that was not the intent of the informal support network?

A different perspective surfaced with two learners who were married to each other and who both fit the description of nontraditional learners. This afforded me the opportunity to gain a different perspective of each of the learners' perspective on the impact of their informal support network. Both learners addressed spousal support; however ironically, they shared two different points of view. As they each conveyed experiences and described the impact of their informal support network, they expressed differences of opinion regarding the impact of that support, and their experiences as both a sender and receiver of support.

The wife had previously attempted to obtain a degree, but lacked the support from her immediate family that she needed in order to be successful. When she began her program, she was single and living alone. She recalled her experiences in a dual mode. First, the tone of her voice was initially one of almost a defeatist attitude with a negative demeanor. During this phase of the interview her nonverbal body language was obvious. She failed to maintain eye contact. She started by looking around with her eyes darting from one object in the room to the next. She also fidgeted constantly in her chair. She sat partly slumped over with her shoulders rounded. This was most noticeable when she recalled her initial unpleasant venture into the education process.

> **My parents thought it was foolish to pursue a degree. After all, as long as you are a hard worker, why do you need some piece of paper saying you are smart, that doesn't make sense? All of my brothers were very successful craftsmen in their own field, except for one; my younger brother went to school to be an engineer. At the time, he really didn't have that big of an influence on me, but he did try. His encouragement was the only support I received from my family at all, both then and now. (Melissa)**

Subsequently, in the context of that family environment, she stepped away from her educational journey and began a career. She basically followed the lead from her family, which was an example of the informal support network in action. Twenty-two years later she met her husband who was pursuing his degree, and he encouraged her to quit her job and return to school to earn her degree as well. As she described this in the interview, her tone changed from a negative to a positive one, which sounded upbeat. Her nonverbal body language noticeably changed as well. She sat up more erect, maintained eye contact, and spoke with confidence.

Her husband had already enjoyed success in obtaining his degree for his chosen field. During his interview, he stated that his desire to better himself even further led to his decision to also pursue a graduate degree, regardless of his personal circumstances or surroundings. His own desire to get another degree and his need for an informal support network were not the same as his wife's, at least not initially.

> **I believe that an individual is responsible for themselves and only themselves and they are a direct result of what they do and should be the person of responsibility. (Martin)**

This statement, along with his physical demeanor and his nonverbal body language, which appeared stoic without much expression, and arrow straight posture, created an impression of great determination and internal drive. He was studying for a Masters degree in sociology. He knew what he wanted and was not going to be deterred from achieving his goal. However, his stoic façade softened as he described his personal journey and mentioned his wife's name in a positive and loving manner. He went beyond simply describing love and emotion as he expressed admiration and mutual respect for the assistance that they had given each other. When he was reflecting on the concept of individual responsibility for one's education, he stopped and shared the following example that showed the importance of his wife's support when he was ill and felt pressured to complete a research paper.

> **When a student takes on the responsibility of a course, they are obligated to do their best job to complete the work in the most effective and efficient manner, regardless of the circumstances in their personal life. For example, I was horribly ill with the flu, one of the worst bouts ever I think on record, but with the help of my wife, nursing me back to health and looking up some of my research articles for me, I was able to get the paper submitted on time and earned an A for my efforts. (Martin)**

The learner expressed a belief that he was more than capable of completing his degree on his own, but statements such as the aforementioned sentiment suggested that on some level his wife was an invaluable source of support, regardless of the type of support she gave.

The results of both interviews with the husband and wife further highlighted the difference that the informal support network had on each of them. The far reaching effects of the informal support network were also highlighted over the lapsed period of time between the wife's earlier educational journey which was stopped due to negative support from her immediate family, and the continuation of her education as a result of positive support from her husband.

Chapter 5

Themes and Sub-themes

The central question establishing the framework for this book was the meaning of the lived experiences of nontraditional learners embedded in informal support networks as they continue their educational journeys or are at the threshold of their educational journeys? The themes identified from the interviews and my own personal experiences revealed that the nontraditional learner was impacted either positively or negatively due to their informal support network depending on their levels of perception and awareness. As I was reflecting upon the time I spent with my nontraditional learners, I began to analyze what they had to say, and I noticed five themes or patterns emerged. It is possible that as the reader, you may relate to some of these themes:

1. Learners experienced their informal support network as having an expandable boundary.

2. Learners experienced their informal support network as varying in strength and influence.

3. Learners experienced their informal support network as having the capacity to magnify the qualities for success they already possessed.

4. Learners experienced their informal support network as

having the ability to expand their capacity to meet the many challenges faced.

5. Learners experienced their informal support network as an evolutionary process throughout the educational journey.

Theme I: Participants Experienced their Informal Support Network As Having an Expandable Boundary

There was a center of support from the immediate family that spread further out at times. This occurred whether the learners perceived it as positive or negative. The support began to expand and gain momentum as their return to the classroom became a reality and was understood by friends and acquaintances beyond the immediate family. The informal support network was not limited to strictly immediate family. Several of the learners stated that their informal support network had expanded to include not only their family members but also, lifelong friends, personal mentors, colleagues, co-workers, and God.

The process of acknowledging support had powerful implications for the learners. This empowered them as they recognized the support they received and began to understand what it encompassed. Support included various activities, such as lawn care, taking care of children, limiting the time commitments at work, proofreading and assisting in the location of research materials. This may not, in and of itself ensure the successful completion of a degree program, but the removal of pressure, either real or perceived, benefited the nontraditional learners. Additionally, acknowledging the support they received may have in part become a self-imposed acceptance of guilt. However, this guilt may have acted as a motivator by imposing on the nontraditional learners the need to succeed in order not to let their informal support network down or disappoint those individuals who had given them support.

Many of the nontraditional learners shared recollections of how their informal support network grew and sometimes caught them off guard. Again, depending upon the feedback received, their surprise could be viewed as either a major advantage or a major disadvantage to the learner. Regardless of how they reacted, when they received this support it had a significant impact on them.

One learner contrasted an experience she had when she first returned to college while in one relationship with her experiences in another relationship.

> Many years ago, I wanted to go to college for two reasons, to be able to get a better job and for a sense of personal satisfaction. I came from a large family where very few even graduated high school, much less college. I wanted to be better than that and get out of the mindset that college was not important. However, when I told my then husband, who did not have a college education either, he laughed and made fun of me. Well, I thought that was that, I still wanted to go, but I could tell he was not going to be any help. What really caught me off guard was a week or two later when we were at his family's house for a party and everyone in his family were asking me why I needed to go back to school and thought it was a big joke, of course at my expense. I really felt and always will that they felt intimidated by the fact that I wanted to better myself. (Lisa)

Her nonverbal body language showed that she was initially tense while describing her ex-husband and his family's response to her announcement, but then it changed, as she appeared relieved and happy when describing the later experience with her fiancé.

> Years and an ex-husband later, I was with my fiancé and I was merely thinking out loud about going back to college. Well, that was all it took, he was transformed before my eyes into an oversized cheerleader encouraging me. Then my kids joined into the act, they were very proud of their Mom for going back to school. Before I knew it, when their friends would come over to play, they were talking about me going back to college. It made me feel that I could go back and be successful, but in all honesty, it gave me a sense of pressure and responsibility that I had to succeed in order not to disappoint my family and friends. (Lisa)

One man recalled his astonishment over the effect the word of his impending return to college, as he phrased it, "spreading like a wildfire" through his family and friends. The wildfire helped keep him motivated and focused on moving in the right direction even when the flame started to waver at times.

> I think you really have to have a passion to go back to school and want to advance yourself, I think that if you do not do that, it creates unhappiness and regret later on in life. My family got behind me from the very beginning, offering words of encouragement, even from some of my aunts and uncles who I didn't even tell, but apparently my other family members told them. Before I knew it, old family friends were coming up to me congratulating me on my decision. I knew at that instant that I was making the right decision and felt empowered by their support. This enabled me to realize one of my primary goals in life ever since I became a freshman in college was to get my Ph.D. (Charles)

Another male learner brought a different insight to this topic of expanding boundaries of the support he received. Even though he stated that his wife was a strong force in his life in many ways, he expressed the importance of support from a different aspect. He felt that this was equally, if not more, influential and crucial to his success, not only in the classroom, but also life in general.

> All through my life, I have always had the feeling that I could do anything that I put my mind to, and I still believe that. But, at the same time, I am not ignorant or conceited enough to believe that I could have accomplished any of my successes in life without the help and guidance of God. Whenever I started a new part of my life, I would pray and ask for direction and help from My Maker. After that, whenever I felt I had His blessing and direction, I would proceed on knowing that nothing or nobody could stop me, with or without anybody's help or approval. I was somewhat deficient and in more plain language I would say I have a need and desire to better myself not only for

financial remuneration but also for personal satisfaction knowing that I can do it somewhat on my own. (Martin)

One of the women shared memories of what happened to her when her informal support network took action. She was "fortunate," as she phrased it, to have had the chance to be surrounded by both love and support from her family and friends who had one goal, to see her succeed. The expanded support network demonstrated various techniques while simultaneously maintaining the solitary focus of assisting her by removing as many obstacles as they could. She gratefully accepted this support, manifested in various forms. She stated that it "made all of the difference in the world." She provided the following example of a self-professed support group. She said that her only regret was that all of their names could not appear on her college degree.

> I guess there was a point where I decided I wanted to do something more in my life. My family backed my decision to return to school with words of encouragement, little notes telling me how proud they were of me, and a wonderful good luck dinner at the beginning of my first semester back. My friends at my job made some suggestions as to what I should major in to help benefit me the most at my job and for my future career path. Their input and support was just as important to me as that of my family because each touched a different part of me. My family touched my heart and the support from my friends and co-workers touched my head and made me really contemplate what would affect my future the most. I am forever in their debt. (Rachael)

It was not uncommon for the learners to look back on their support network's contribution to their success and express appreciation. One learner recalled how the boundary of his informal support network expanded in a very short time.

> I had moved to West Virginia where my wife's family lived and at the time had a Bachelor's in Social Work. There really was not a lot of opportunity with just that type of degree. I developed an interest in Administration and knew that a Master's in Business Administration would give me

a lot more opportunities for advancement, so I decided to go on and pursue a higher level of education. As soon as my in-laws heard about it, they were trying to line up jobs for me already before I had my Master's degree started. I was getting calls from my father-in-law's company offering me a job, pending the completion of my MBA, talk about pressure. But, it did help, not only were my wife and kids pulling for me, but my in-laws, and future employer were on my side as well, how could I have failed? (Keith)

The concept of "enriching" may have offered important insight into the contribution of the informal support network. It could be a solitary journey for nontraditional adult learners placed in an environment, which was more suited to traditional learners. The informal support network provided a sounding board, a place to vent, a mirror to reflect thoughts, and help to process those thoughts. This resulted in the learners gaining deeper learning both of subject content and also about them. A more refined, realistic, and optimistic sense of self emerged from this enriched environment provided by the informal support network.

Voices from the past could and often have had profound impact on individuals; nontraditional learners were no different. Immediate family and friends, as cited in this book, could contribute greatly to the success or failure of nontraditional learners. But, the reminiscence of one learner emphasized the far-reaching capacity and impact of the past on the present. In addition, he desired to make those who he perceived to be key or important members of his informal support network proud of his accomplishments and progress. This could be attributed to experiencing gratitude or a sense of debt/owing.

> I had personal ambitions and goals for myself; I wanted to be the Head of School. I think that was what made it all possible. But goals and ambitions were only part of it. My wife was an invaluable resource and my personal cheerleader, but perhaps one of the most influential forces in my success was my mentor, a man that I respected greatly and who I wanted to be proud of me. He called upon my entry in the doctoral studies program after having lost contact with him for about six years after my deployment

> in the military overseas; he called and offered wonderful words of wisdom in my opinion. The input, counsel, and verbal prodding I received from him were both inspirational and extremely beneficial throughout my entire course of study and when I finally completed my Ph.D. His opinion of my accomplishments and me were and will continue to remain a high priority of mine. (Adam)

One learner started college when she was 45 and graduated with her Bachelors degree at the age of 49. She recalled that a supervisor whom she described as her boss, mentor, friend, and confidant had encouraged her to return to college. She frequently told her supervisor that she felt she was too stupid to go to college. However, the supervisor worked with her, giving her assignments and challenges that built up her self-esteem.

> Because of his efforts, I was able to prove to myself that I was intelligent enough to pursue an education and be successful. Without his gentle yet persuasive approach to my stubbornness, I know as sure as I am sitting here that I would never have even registered for my first college class, much less graduate in the top twenty in my class. Now that is help and friendship that you can't buy. (Melissa)

However, a number of the research participants stated that they were reluctant to allow themselves to expand and embrace their educational potential. The learners found that their informal support network helped them redefine who they were in a manner that enhanced their self efficacy and gave them greater confidence to take on the long-term commitment to advance their education. They acknowledged that they feared criticism and the loss of control. While they needed support, they did not welcome the perceived assistance and support that was offered. This was done in an effort not to offend those in their informal support network. They feared that the time it would take to involve others might have taken them away from their focus on their educational journey.

The feeling of being independent/self-reliant had both positive and negative connotations. The sense of being independent had some beneficial attributes for the learners, but it limited the amount of resources at their disposal. The learners who stated that they considered themselves to be independent or self-reliant, often also acknowledged the importance of the presence and support they received from those individuals and family members in their informal support network. Therefore, they highlighted the struggle between wanting independence/self-reliance and needing support.

One man recalled how he did not welcome experiencing the support from his family and extended family due to his fear and anxiety over the future and not wanting to hurt his loved ones.

> At the time that I was going to college I was on active duty in the Marine Corps. Also, I was trying to help raise my daughter and salvage a quickly deteriorating marriage, which ended in divorce. A little voice kept telling me to do everything I could now, and that included getting my education done as quickly as possible before my retirement from the Corps. Even though my Grandmother and Mom supported me, and in all honesty, my Wife a little, I really didn't want anyone to know or try to help. It was a rough time for me and I really just wanted to be by myself and get it done without feeling that I had to talk or see anyone else. It was my way of handling the situation. (Daniel)

Another learner had a different reason for wanting to keep her return to college to earn a degree a secret until she had completed a few semesters.

> My husband really pushed me to go back to school. I will forever be grateful to him for doing that. Not only did I get the opportunity to get an education that helped me get a job that I really wanted, it helped to strengthen our marriage. I didn't have to worry about him criticizing me when I had trouble with my classes, which I did. He only offered me help and the proverbial kick in the backside. Unfortunately, my family all have these really great college degrees that seemed to come so easy to them. I knew then like I know now that they wouldn't understand that I was having problems, I am just not a naturally brainy person like my brothers and sister. (Rachel)

Time is a very precious commodity; this was very obvious for one nontraditional learner as he experienced the time crunch with juggling family, career, and education. To further complicate the picture, the perceived loss of control by the learner was convoluted more by the loss of his job and significantly increased financial pressures.

> Don't get me wrong, I love my family deeply and will forever hold their help to me in my heart, but at times it could get to be too much. Their idea of help was to come around to help with tasks around the house, or they did things with the kids, and that was great. But, when they initially found out about me losing my job, good grief, I thought I had a new arm and leg. My brothers were around all of the time trying to do things or line up interviews for me. It quickly got to the point that I couldn't get my work on my courses done or I was so frustrated that I couldn't function. I know to this day that they meant well, but sometimes too much is too much. (Mark)

In Mark's case, the presence of the informal support network carried with it an assumed responsibility to either accept the expanded version of his support network with many members or to attempt to keep it at a smaller, more intimate level. This decision was based upon the learner's needs and his perceptions about how the expanded informal support network would impact him.

Theme 2: Participants Experienced Their Informal Support Network As Varying in Strength and Influence

The learners did not experience their informal support network as a constant and unwavering presence. The interviews in this area provided the following results, which show the varying support received by the learners. The results have been categorized into four sub-themes:

Sub-Theme 1: The Power of an Informal Support Network

The concept of the informal support network functioning as a force enabling the nontraditional learners to succeed was a powerful one with the ability to propel the learner to success in the academic setting which he or she might not otherwise experience. The learners who stated that they felt or perceived this enabling force experienced it not only as a sense of knowing that they had the ability to achieve a task, but even greater as the ability to continue pursuing their educational goals. This enabling ability can lead nontraditional learners to push themselves towards the next level of success.

However, the simple presence of an informal support network did not guarantee success. What the informal support network did was give the nontraditional learners a perceived or real sense of being influenced or supported regardless of how the support was manifested. This network had the potential to either facilitate an environment conducive to nontraditional learners' success or to act as a negative force hindering their progress or attempt at an education at all.

One woman commented that she felt competitive with her husband who was also pursuing a degree. She said that this spirit of competition and support helped sustain her through some rather challenging times when she went back to college.

> It is that competitiveness that drives me, I am extremely competitive, extremely stubborn, and I guess you could say I was in love with him and didn't want to let him down. But at the same time, I didn't want to lose, not even to my husband. We have constantly laughed at how we are helping each other by motivating each of us to do better while driving each other crazy at the same time, now that is true love and I wouldn't trade it for the world. (Melissa)

Besides being students with full professional lives, some of the learners were also soldiers in the military. Although these nontraditional learners felt that being a soldier carried many well known assumptions and stereotypes about how they should behave, they also knew that it did not mean that they were immune to hurt and emotional pain simply because they were soldiers. This was woven into the story recalled rather painfully from one man who was surprised by the strength and faith in his family and how they continued to help him during their own troubled times.

> After being in the Army for a couple of years, I quickly realized how much I needed to finish my education if I wanted to get promoted. After some discussions with my wife, parents, and my superior officers, I enrolled in college. Attempting to juggle all of my responsibilities was difficult to say the least, but I could always count on my wife and mother for the shoulder to lean on or that home cooked meal to pep me up. I remember during finals, everyone seemed on edge, but I was totally absorbed in my own world and how my wife and mom were really trying to help me even more. It wasn't until after finals that I was told about Mom's cancer, she didn't want to distract me from my duties and college. After months of illness and finally Mom losing her battle to cancer, I used her strength to keep me going during my grieving and subsequently, attaining my dream of a Ph.D. I believe she is proud of me. (Adam)

The oldest woman of the group recalled how roles were reversed when she announced her return to the classroom, this time not as a teacher, but as a student. As a mother, she was one providing the support for her grown children in college, and now she was also a student.

> You have to understand my mentality going into this new phase in my life. I was sixty-two years old and going back to college to get my PhD in education, my lifelong career and passion. Professors that were younger than some of my own children were teaching me. I laughingly told my children about this and before I knew what was happening, they started to do or say little things for me. It was almost like our roles were reversed parent to child and child to the parental role. They started supporting me in ways that I had done to them two decades earlier. Without my dear husband there to help me, I then felt that I could lean on my children and have the strength and courage to keep going. I am truly blessed and very fortunate to have such loving kids. (Sarah)

Age is not an indicator of the amount or level of support that the nontraditional learner needs or could receive. In this particular instance, this woman had the opportunity to experience something that many people also desired, the unsolicited love and devotion of a child.

> Due to some bad decisions on my part when I was younger, I did not have the opportunity to go to college when most others my age were, I was raising a beautiful little boy at the time by myself. Two years ago, I decided it was time for me to go back to college and try to better myself so that I could provide for George, my little man and me. At this time, he was five years old. Only being able to take classes in the evening, it has taken me considerable more time to complete my degree. But, something truly wonderful has happened to me as a result of this experience with my education. George and I have become so much closer. He has really helped me in little precious and innocent ways that make me know that all of this time and work is truly worth it. He may be the smallest member of my family, but I know if I didn't have him to keep me going that I would drop out right now. (Glenda)

Sub-Theme 2: The Manifestation of the Informal Support Network

The learners demonstrated how the support was manifested and also varied in structure and strength, while at the same time, it wavered from a positive to a negative force or vice versa. Various levels of awareness that had not yet been realized by the learners surfaced as a result of the actions or inactions of the informal support network. However, what was the essence of this support in the perceived experience of the nontraditional learners? What made this support obvious to them? How did it present itself as a positive or negative influence? The following recollections of the nontraditional learner's responses demonstrated how their informal support network manifested itself.

Several learners discussed how the discernible emotional support they received became obvious in many different modes from their informal support network, and as a result the learners viewed the support positively.

> One of my best friends was very enthusiastic about my

> decision to pursue my Ph.D. She said if I wanted to do it and if this is something that has always been a goal of mine, then I really need to go for it. It really helped to have somebody who is a good friend like that where I respect her intelligence and drive to really encourage me in that way. In terms of emotional support, I would say that was one example. (Charles)

Sometimes family support came from the most unlikely of people according to several learners. When this occurred, it was welcomed, included various forms of support, and was viewed as a positive experience.

> My older sister, who I never really got along with when we were growing up or in all honesty that much since we both moved out of the house and started our own lives. One day, she really surprised me. I knew that she had her Bachelors degree and that was great. But my first attempt at college was a disaster due to my family situation. After I met my fiancé, I started considering a return. I heard that my sister was working on her Masters degree in education, and I decided to give her a call. I really don't know why I did, but I am glad I did. My sister basically told me that maybe I shouldn't try it again since I failed at it the first time. Failed! Well, now not only am I going to get my Bachelors, I am going to get my Masters as well. So, every time she calls, with either good intentions or not, I use it as motivation to press on. But, the one good thing for sure that came from this experience is that I am talking to my sister, and in her own way I believe deep down she wants me to succeed, this has brought us together again. (Lisa)

Sometimes, even the most independent individual needed some help and understanding from others in their lives. This man displayed emotion as he recollected this experience.

> I am a staunch believer in an individual's own ability to do whatever they put their minds to. I do believe that I did succeed in my prior educational goals because of my dedication and hard work and that I will again in my current course of study. With that being said, the love and

> support of my wife has made my life by far easier with her by my side versus going solo. Perhaps the most profound demonstration is her ability to know that time is needed and she does her best to give me as much time as possible, even making sacrifices herself in order for this to take place. (Martin)

One man related an incident concerning how his wife's second job provided support for him to focus on his education.

> I told you before that my wife, kids, and mother-in-law had been and continue to be absolutely wonderful to me throughout this entire time that I have gone back to school. My wife especially has been my biggest supporter. In order to try to allow me to spend more time on my classes and study time, she took on a second job so that I could cut back on my hours at work and not feel that I was letting the family down. But what really gets me is that when she gets home after me now, she still asks if there is anything she can do to help me. I only hope that I can do something nearly as kind and loving for her someday. (Mark)

Sub-Theme 3: How the Realized Support Impacted the Women

The women who experienced negative feedback from their informal support network explained how it affected their decision to continue in their educational endeavors. Three of the women who contemplated a return to the college environment for the first time experienced a negative response from their informal support network that initially acted as a barrier to their success. Although each of the women initially continued to pursue their education after a few courses, the negativity from the informal support network or lack of support was so great that they later decided to abandon their efforts.

> I had tried to take classes and the people in my immediate family at the time were not very supportive. I received negative comments including them telling me that it wasn't worth it, or I couldn't do it. I think that was very detrimental to me. Subsequently, I decided to drop the

classes because I got tired of people telling me that I was wasting my time. (Lisa)

The perception that their family would always be there has been dispelled many times by the learners. This example described how a single mother was basically left on her own without the benefit of the support that she needed and desired.

> Both of my brothers were negative towards my decision to return to college, mainly because they were able to make it on their own without a degree. My mother would babysit my son but that was about all of the support she gave. I started back to college the first time 10 years ago but had to quit because I needed tutoring and had trouble without the support of my family getting the help I needed with my schoolwork and taking care of my son. (Glenda)

Another woman recalled a rather unpleasant experience when she asked for some assistance from her parents.

> My parents thought that it was foolish. Other than my younger brother, the rest of my family told me that I was on a wild goose chase and that I would never do it. But, my younger brother was a true model and lifesaver to me. (Melissa)

The incidence of leaving a job has been traditionally viewed as a negative experience. However, in this case one woman turned a negative experience into a positive and beneficial experience with the help of a former co-worker.

> After working in several departments where I worked and feeling like I would never be able to advance into a management position, I decided to go back and get a degree so that I would be more employable. The great thing of that experience was that I developed a deep friendship with a co-worker at the time and we began helping each other and encouraging each other to do well in school. (Lisa)

Another facet of this issue that emerged because of the behavioral patterns between the genders was the perceived attitudes the women experienced by those individuals who formed their informal support network. Of the five women, the three oldest, ranging from 38 to 67 years of age, expressed a sense of biased attitudes and prejudice from their families' attitudes in the treatment they received. This was in direct contrast to the attitudes towards their male siblings who wished to pursue their education. One woman stated:

> My younger brother who graduated from college, he supported my decision. My father told me that I was too stupid for college. Yet, my brother was in college at the time. Now, if that wasn't a sexist statement, even by my own father, what is? (Melissa)

The oldest woman shared the story of how the male members of her family as far back as her grandfather had all graduated from the University of Virginia. In her words, it was a family tradition. However, when she wanted to enroll at the University of Virginia to earn her Bachelor's degree her mother supported her decision, but her father was totally against it. When she successfully completed her Bachelor's degree, she found that her father and brothers would not speak of her college success. Even decades later, the perceived attitude from the male family members remained the same even as she was beginning to pursue her doctorate degree.

The third woman who experienced bias from her informal support network stated that no one in her family had a degree and they had been successful without one. Her family never told her that she should go to college and that if she did she had to do everything on her own without anyone's help. She told her family that they did not know what they were talking about, but they did not provide support.

The remaining two women stated that they only received\positive feedback from their family support network when they told them that they were contemplating a return to college.

> When I told my kids that I was going back to school at night, without me saying a word, they got up and starting cleaning the house and did the dishes. When I finally caught up to the whirling dervishes, I asked them why the sudden burst of energy and cleaning streak. I was promptly told by my children that if I could work and go back to school that

> the least they could do was help around the house. How could I fail with love like that? I only wish I would have gone back earlier and gotten out of my housework. (Lisa)

One woman joked that her husband was to blame for her decision to return to school.

> My husband was a big encouragement. He kept telling me that I was doing a good job and that I should be an English teacher, so he actually was the one who put the idea in my head. (Rachael)

Another woman recalled how she received her initial support from her kids and her husband. However, later the same night, the support from her children ended and they begged her not to go back to school at all.

> My husband reacted in a way that I never could have imagined; he made me dinner. This was a scary process in itself, considering that he had never done anything like that before for me in five years of marriage. After eating his homemade dinner, which wasn't too bad, he told me that he was going to start making dinner for the kids and him and that I didn't have to worry about making dinners. After some pleading from my kids, an agreement was made that he would do dinner on the nights I had evening classes and I would do the rest. Everyone was happy then, especially me. (Melissa)

Another woman said that initially it was her fiancé's idea and at the time she did not think that it would be possible for her to go back to school with work and children at home. When she finally made the decision, she consulted with him to get his input.

> I wanted to get my fiancé's advice because I knew that he would tell me that I was making the right choice and his words let me know that he supported my decision and me. It was as though I could not make the decision without confirming that he would be there to support me along the way, because I did not feel confident in my ability to succeed on my own. (Lisa)

Sub-Theme 4: How the Realized Support Impacted the Men

There was a noticeable disparity between the men and women's experiences. The men recognized their own drive and motivation. They implemented their informal family support network as a compliment to their internal drive and as a way to clear their thoughts in order to focus on their education. However, this support did manifest itself in many different ways.

The impact of the support one man's wife provided by telling him that she knew what he wanted to accomplish and giving him the freedom to pursue his goal of obtaining a degree, allowed him to proceed without feeling as though he was being selfish.

> I am secure in my family environment in that I know that my wife can fill the void of me having to take time off to do my studies. She understands that anything that moves me ahead moves our family ahead. Having that type of mental freedom allowed me to focus on my classes instead of having gnawing feelings of guilt or thinking that I should be doing something with my family at that time versus sitting in a classroom. (Mark)

Another man expressed how he was impacted by the support his wife provided when she went to the library and conducted research for him, and then proofread his work. Her support helped him to feel more comfortable asking her for help and aided in his overall success.

> By taking this approach, it made my wife feel more involved in the process and enabled me to proceed on further with fewer barriers. She became an active partner in my learning process. Not only did we work together on my degree but it also brought us closer together as friends and partners. This helped our relationship grow even stronger and deeper. (Adam)

Another man who experienced some negativity stated that his friend's support made his return to college to earn his degree a good experience, but then he had difficulties when his wife was not supportive of his decision. Eventually he withdrew from school.

> I know one friend who went back to school and it caused some dissention in their marriage. He withdrew because he didn't want to overcome the negative feelings of his family. Dana was, well I don't know what her problem was, but she just wanted no part of him going back to finish his degree. So it is a very difficult thing to do if you do not have the support from your family and friends. (Charles)

Another man shared how his friend's inability to finish his degree program created a strain in their relationship because he [the learner] was still able to pursue his degree and had the support of his family. The nature of the friend's support was negative, but it impacted the learner in a way that made him want to prove to his friend that it was worth pursuing even without his spouse's support.

> I tried to show my friend that you could have a family, career, and go back to school, and how much easier it was and could be for him if only his wife would help him or at least stop being against it. Unfortunately, all this did was bring on bad feelings between him and I and it cost me a good friend. But it did increase the love and admiration I have for my wife and family. I guess you don't know how good you have it until you see someone that doesn't have it. (Charles)

Theme 3: Participants Experienced Their Informal Support Network as Having the Capacity to Magnify the Qualities for Success They Already Possessed

It was not necessary for nontraditional learners to attempt to reinvent themselves merely because they were older, or had been out of school for several years, or for other reasons. Obviously, if the individual felt strong enough to attempt or to enter the college environment in order to better themselves or to learn a new skill or knowledge set, their will and desire was evident. However, this wave of enthusiasm could quickly recede, leaving them with the ability and tools to succeed, but lacking the necessary motivation. This was where the informal support network began to have a significant influence on nontraditional learners, either in a positive or negative manner.

The concept of fear of failure could be channeled into a positive experience and act as an impetus to turn potential failure into success and a prosperous future. However, when this fear of failure was facilitated and nurtured by the informal support network, it successfully challenged nontraditional learners. Those who successfully converted this negative support into a positive force were able to use that fuel to push them forward and have a positive effect on those around them. They saw themselves as possessing the confidence and ability to achieve their goals and objectives in the academic realm.

One man showed how the impact of the informal support network increased his will and desire to succeed and complete his degree.

> I may have considered not returning to college after graduating with my Bachelors twelve years previously, if my wife and family really worked on me not to go back; luckily they didn't. But, if I didn't want to go back to school, there is no way they could have persuaded me to go back to school. The desire was already there. My wife and kids really acted as my cheerleaders or as my Father's Day card said, Happy Father's Day from your biggest and loudest fans. Now that is what I call support. (Martin)

Sometimes the influence of a member of the informal support network can be present, even when the nontraditional learner is unaware of it. In those instances, many times actions spoke much louder than words. In this case, a member of the informal support network helped to further inspire and motivate this participant.

> I had wanted to go back to school for a number of years, but my previous college experience was not that great. I didn't have any kind of support, well at least any kind of good support from my ex-husband or family. But, after meeting my now fiancé, I saw how he was working hard on his degree and the joy he had whenever he would complete another one of his courses. I wanted that joy and excitement back inside of me again. He literally helped to fuel what was already there, my desire to go back to

school, if for no other reason than for myself and a sense of self-accomplishment. (Lisa)

One woman fondly recounted how her former supervisor frequently told her that she could go back to school and be successful. The participant resisted it. However, the persistence of the supervisor prevailed.

> My former supervisor was always telling me that I should go back to college and I kept on telling him that I couldn't do it, I didn't have the brains for it. But, I now know why he was the supervisor, he tricked me. He would give me assignments requiring a great deal of research and would make the projects I would be involved with more challenging each and every time. Then, it happened. He told me what he had been doing. He was building up my confidence without me even realizing it. He had the ability to see my potential even when I didn't, I will be eternally grateful. (Melissa)

One man was a retired career Marine Corps. Sergeant. He knew his duties, performed them to his utmost, and was recognized for his efficiency and effectiveness numerous times. However, while he felt that he had the ability to get his degree, he felt that he lacked the critical thinking skills to succeed. This was one reason why he opted not to take advantage of OCTS training. His Commanding Officer attempted to influence his future.

> My CO was one of the toughest men I have ever met. He commanded loyalty of his troops and he received it willingly because he was a good man. But, he reprimanded me for not accepting a slot in Officers Candidate Training School; I didn't agree with him, I didn't believe that I could do it. I didn't think that I had the critical thinking skills necessary to make a good officer. However, he kept working on me. He never got me in OCTS, but he did keep on stressing my ability to me and finally got me to enroll in my first college course. (Daniel)

Theme 4: Participants Experienced Their Informal Support Network as Having the Ability to Expand Their Capacity to Meet the Many Challenges Faced

This theme focused on the participants' capacity to expand on the various forms and levels of support from their informal support network that provided them opportunities to succeed. Although the nature of support that these nontraditional learners received varied greatly, not many distinctive differences were found to suggest that gender was a factor in the amount of positive support received. As an informal consensus, nine of the learners agreed that one of the most important benefits of the support received was encouragement. While this characteristic was defined in many different ways by each of the learners, they all described encouragement as manifested by offers of verbal, emotional, or physical assistance.

The concept of changing self-understanding was also powerful. Most people did not know what the outer edge of their ability was until they were pushed to test it. As the nontraditional learners' motivation was enhanced through the sense of owing and their desire to repay those in their informal support network, the nontraditional learners were pushed to achieve things they would not have otherwise achieved. As a result, their self-understanding was altered. At first, this was achieved at a superficial level and emerged from the encouragement of their informal support network. Phrases like, "I believe in you," "you can do this," and "you are smarter than you realize" were initially used by the informal support network because they saw it as an easy way to be supportive. However, as the participants were bolstered by other motivating and support factors which emerged from their informal support network, they actually began to achieve things they had not thought they were capable of achieving. The resulting modification of their self-understanding became more profound and permanent. This notion of an altering self-understanding stood in initial opposition with those participants who talked about their personal confidence levels. They saw themselves as able to achieve their goals, but they also acknowledged that their informal support network made the process more fulfilling and richer.

One learner seemed amazed by some revelations in the interview.

The expression on her face revealed her amazement even more than her words.

> I received verbal encouragement from my family when I wasn't doing well or felt like I was not going to receive a successful grade. The verbal pep talks really helped me get through the depths of some of my doldrums. Really, it's amazing to think what just a few words can do to uplift a person. (Rachael)

For the most part, the informal support network consisted of adults. But in some cases, the little ones in the learners' lives surprised them with an unusual sense of maturity and wisdom. The following remembrance by one woman describes this.

> I received not only words of encouragement, but I was given a little book on reflections about how to deal with change and it can be very good. Many times I would re-read certain passages, but I always start with the dedication on the inside jacket of the book. It is a message from my kids telling me that they are proud of me and that they want to grow up to be like me. I am sorry; it is hard not to start to tear up when I think of that. (Lisa)

It was very beneficial when the nontraditional learners received positive reinforcement in the form of telling them that they could accomplish a task. However, sometimes humor also provided support and acted as a motivational factor. While providing support, this learner's informal support network had a positive effect on her, but the approach used to benefit her were different than more serious approaches.

> My husband was very encouraging as far as supporting me with time, helping me study, and setting up my school books, classes and so forth. My friends were great also. They threw me a World's Oldest Student party to celebrate my return to college complete with a cane and a cushion for me to sit on. That is a memory that helped to get me through some rough times, but one that I truly cherish. (Melissa)

Insight has emerged from the research on this topic that went beyond the educational realm. The support received from the informal support network had far reaching effects. In most cases it was a positive experience; however, in some it had negative consequences, which has been conveyed in this book.

In the following recollection by one man, what started as an educational journey turned into a spiritual and an emotional occurrence, one that he will not forget?

> My wife encouraged me to pursue a Master's degree so that I could move forward in my career. She has given me confidence to reach heights and more important, inner parts of my soul and my being that I thought was long since dead. After many years of failure and mistakes, I am forever indebted to this lady. This rejuvenation of my spirit prompted me to continue on with my Master's degree and apply and secure a new position with the commitment of finishing my degree within the next year. (Mark)

Previous relationships evolved to something unique and special. The changes demonstrated how the informal support network was flexible and adapted to the individual needs or desires of the learner.

> My wife and brother were a big encouragement to me when I was trying to get my bachelors degree. My wife was great, it went from telling me that I could do it, to telling me that because of my dedication and making sacrifices for the family that she decided to go back to school herself. I think I was more proud of myself for that then for actually going back to school. My brother was great too. He would call and offer to do the little things for me, like research papers or final exams; you know little things and would laugh. But, I was so involved in my classes, that it took me awhile to realize that the lawn was getting mowed and that the firewood had been cut and stacked for the winter. If it wouldn't have been for my little girl telling me, my brother wasn't going to say anything at all. To think that I used to pick on that overgrown ox. (Keith)

The forms of support manifested itself in different modes, sometimes as a friendly word, helping around the house, and sometimes it took the form of smiles and laughter. The following was a humorous example of how the roles of subordinates changed to that of a standup comedian.

> **When I decided to continue my education, I consulted with my wife and two colleagues and they were all very encouraging. But encouragement only goes so far. Whenever my energy level would start to run down or I would start to doubt or question myself, my wife would remind me about some of the challenges that I had faced during my military career and how I had overcome those and learned from them. My colleagues were great. They would constantly tease me about whether they should salute me or bow before me since I was getting my doctorate. Then they would talk to me about insignificant occurrences when I would stress out in an effort to get me to relax and refocus my energy. But I interpreted it as a sign of good-natured acceptance and encouragement to continue on towards completion of the degree. (Adam)**

One man recalled how the assistance from his supervisors was welcome and accepted, but explained that they had their own agenda for offering the unsolicited assistance to help further their own work environment.

> **My supervisors are encouraging me and also they are trying to see to it that I receive some kind of reward down the road for this. I really believe that my supervisor and president want me to succeed, but I think they have their own agenda set up for me when I finish my degree. After working there for over ten years now, I am being groomed for upper management; I just lack the required degree for them to be able to fill in the box on the application. They are my friends, but they also have a business to run, so I believe that their concern and support is to both help themselves and me at the same time and that's ok with me too. (Martin)**

One man described the feedback he received. His support was evident in different manners, but one was clear in that it boosted his self-confidence in his own abilities and desires to succeed. But, what he described as really amazing was his family's ability to deal with his changing needs and wishes as he progressed throughout the educational process.

> Most everyone I consulted told me to go for it and said things like if that is what I want to do, then that is what you should do. I encountered some negativity but it was a very small percentage. Being a Marine at the time, I had the attitude that I could do anything, but once in the classroom, I quickly realized that I was out of my element. I told my brothers and my Grandmother about my feelings, for some reason I felt like I couldn't tell my wife. Anyway, it was like a good cop and bad cop scenario. My Grandmother has always been my biggest fan and my brothers, well being the baby of the bunch, I was always teased and picked on, but all three of my brothers really gave me words of encouragement and told me about how they faced some of their fears. These were sides of them that I had never seen before. But my Grandmother went from this sweet old woman to yelling at me and saying that she was disappointed in me. I couldn't believe it, she was yelling at me, her favorite grandson. But then I listened to what she was saying. She was disappointed in me because I wanted to quit and she expected better of me. She definitely got my attention and it worked. (Daniel)

One benefit of having an informal support network that was mentioned often was receiving assistance with studies. This was mentioned by eight of the research participants, both men and women.

> I received a lot of motivation, and assistance in completing the paperwork; help with research, and with household duties in order for me to be able to focus on my course work. (Lisa)

> I remember that I always received encouragement and help with studying. Whether something needed to be typed or I needed someone to ask me questions or listen to my presentations, she [wife] was willing to do that. (Keith)

> My wife would help me by doing a lot of my research at the library or act as my own personal editor. I honestly

believe that this helped cut probably six months off my completion time but more importantly, it allowed me to use the precious little time I had to actually do the work itself instead of sitting in the library. She was a real lifesaver. (Charles)

Theme 5: Participants Experienced Their Informal Support Network as an Evolutionary Process Throughout the Educational Journey

The word evolutionary characterized the idea of change and adaptation. This final theme emerged as a result of the various interviews and the nontraditional learners' descriptions of how their support began to change and grow. The learners' recollections of how the support they received evolved demonstrated the triumph of the human spirit in face of what at the time appeared to be insurmountable odds. Both the overt messages and perceived messages from the informal support network were interpreted by the learners as motivators, which ultimately aided in their success, despite any negative messages they received. The impact of this support varied for each learner based on the type of support they received. One woman described the nature of support from her informal network as negative, and she described how that impacted her.

A negative informal support network may have been attempting to hold the research participant in a previously defined and limited box of understanding of what he or she could achieve. However, it may have actually reversed the process of the changing and evolving self-concept by turning it in a positive direction. Those learners who were able to resist their family's subculture and succeed even in the face of resistance from family members changed their self-understanding, perhaps in deeply powerful ways. They were proving to themselves that they could break out of the family mold and go beyond its limiting features.

> Although I only received negativity from my family, I tried, but the odds were not in my favor. I just couldn't fight everybody at one time. After my initial withdrawal from college, I started looking at their negativity differently and

eventually it acted as a motivator for me to pursue my degree even more. (Lisa)

Another woman stated that her parents saw no value in her pursuing a degree, which she viewed as negative feedback. The negativity prompted her to go back and get her Master's degree, and then she started to see some changes in their opposition to her college dreams.

> My parents saw no value in a degree. My father kept saying that now that I have a degree I act uppity. Eventually, I just agreed and said that I was uppity now and that I am proud of my degree. This negativity acted as a motivation to go back and pursue my Master's degree. However, as I successfully completed my classes, my mom started to ask what I was learning; when I would tell her, she wouldn't say anything else. But, maybe a couple of days later, she would ask my advice about something that was related to the courses that I just finished. My father never changed, but my mom sure did. (Melissa)

Chapter 6

Conclusion or...Just the Beginning?

"From small beginnings come great things. The distance doesn't matter; it is only the first step that is difficult."

-Marquise du Deffand

The results of the research revealed that all of the research participants were impacted by the nature of the support that they received. The support received, either positive or negative, was utilized to motivate the learner to excel in spite of the informal support network member's intentions. In every case, the learners responded to the nature of the support received and how it impacted them in a way that was ultimately beneficial to their educational journey.

How can you succeed as a nontraditional learner in a world that seemingly is putting up obstacles as fast as you can get past the last one? The richness of the feedback from the learners yields a wealth of guidance to you, the reader, and next generation of nontraditional learners. Some of the barriers to success that were identified in this book can present a great challenge to the nontraditional learner. But, if there is adequate support from your informal support network and other support networks in the collegiate environment, there is potential to decrease some of the barriers to success, there is also great opportunity to take these barriers and turn them into a positive. It is up to you, the reader, to be able to examine your situation and identify any potential barriers that may exist in your life that could either increase or decrease your chance for success, and turn those barriers into opportunities for success. Seek out educational institutes that offer programs to help nontraditional learners integrate into the academic environment. Learn how to request assistance from available resources, either from your informal support network or from the educational institution itself. Most important, realize the opportunities that lay ahead of you, only if you grasp the opportunity and utilize to the fullest extent the resources at your disposal. Don't forget, the resources can be your family, circle of friends, co-workers, and God. But, don't be discouraged; even if on the surface, you perceive that you possess none of these resources or informal support networks, rely on your best and most dependable resource and support network…yourself. Keep one thing in mind, even with the strongest and most reliable informal support network; ultimately, it is your responsibility, the learner to navigate the journey along your own educational journey. Your GPS is your informal support network, however, before that; we had to utilize maps to reach our desired destinations, we had to rely on ourselves. Read this book for what it is intended to do, a model of how other nontraditional learners accomplished their goals. Your own situations are unique unto themselves, yet, very similar to others. You both desired to fulfill your educational needs. This is only the beginning of your journey, not the conclusion. So, prepare yourself for the ups and downs, the emotional highs and lows. But, remain focused on your ultimate goal, no not your degree alone, but the self-satisfaction you achieved, your objective and winning! Pass this book along to those who you feel can help you, all they can say is no at the worst. If they do, thank them for motivating you even more to succeed on your educational journey. Finally, remember you possess the ultimate responsibility to succeed or fail, but you also possess the ability to reach out for assistance. After all, even the Lone Ranger had Tonto. So, what are you waiting for, take control and get started and best of luck to you and your informal support network.

Nontraditional Learner Reference Guide

The following reference guide to success for the nontraditional learner was based on the conveyed lived experiences of successful nontraditional learners in a variety of career fields. This guide can be customized to your individual situation; however, it does not guarantee success automatically. The benefit for you, the learner, is to be able to identify some of the characteristics that you possess that will help to increase your chances for success in the classroom. The rest is up to you. Your drive and motivation to continue your education provides a cornerstone to your educational success. Although these are significant factors that contribute to success, understanding how to manage other influences in your life will help you to develop a strategy to overcome obstacles or build resistance against these underlying factors that inhibit your success.

1. Communicate your needs to your support network
2. Be thick-skinned
3. Be willing to accept the support offered
4. Be self motivated, nurture your own learning process
5. Realize that some support may be negative
6. Learn how to turn a negative into a positive
7. Celebrate your victories, small or large

8. Identify your own learning style

9. Maintain focus

10. Realize the informal support network is important but if its presence is not there, success can still be obtained

Keep in mind that the past is not always destined to repeat itself, but the smart man learns from it and how to avoid the pitfalls and problems that those who went before him experienced. Stay focused and remember that you control your own destiny, no one else, not even you informal support network.

Summary

The entire group of eleven learners made similar statements to show that they all received positive feedback from the various members of their informal support network. However, in conjunction with this positive feedback, four of the eleven learners received some degree of negativity from their informal support network. There was also an obvious disparity between the perceived impressions and experiences between the men and women regarding the informal support networks and how they impacted their educational journey. However, the emotions and perceived impressions of these nontraditional learners yielded a wealth of information about how the informal support network worked on many different levels. Please keep in mind that these experiences may or may not resemble your situation, and that is fine. The important thing is that you recognize the value of the informal support network.

Education is not preparation for life; education is life itself.

~ John Dewey

References

American Heritage Dictionary (2000) *Interdependent definition.* Retrieved on November 3, 2008 from http://dictionary.reference.com/browse/interdependent

Association for Nontraditional Students in Higher Education (ANTSHE). (n.d.). *The constitution of association for nontraditional students in higher education.* Retrieved on January 30, 2006, from html:http://www.antshe.org/Official%20Documents/ANTSHE_Constitution.mht

Bauer, D. & Mott, D. (2001). Life themes and motivations of re-entry students. Journal of Counseling & Development. 68.

Bauman, S., Wang, N., DeLeon, C., Kafentzis, J., Zavala-Lopez, M. & Lindsey, M. (2005). Nontraditional students' service needs and social support resources: A pilot study. Retrieved on November 27, 2005, from http://www.questia.com/PM.qst?action=print&docId=5010964866

Bell, J. (2003). Statistics anxiety: The nontraditional student. *Education, 124(1)* 157-162, 6. Retrieved on December 30, 2005, from http://search.epnet.com/login.aspx?direct=true&db+aph&an=11047184">statisticsanxiety:thenontraditionalstudent.</A>

Benshoff, J. & Lewis, L. (1992). *Nontraditional college students. ERIC Digest.* Ann Arbor, MI: ERIC Clearinghouse on Counseling and Personnel Services. (ERIC Document Reproduction Service No. ED347483)

Bird, J. & Morgan, C. (2003). Adults contemplating university study at a distance: Issues, themes and concerns. *The International Review of Research in Open and Distance Learning, 4,* 1.

Bowen, M. (2004). *Bowen Theory.* Retrieved on April 30, 2006, from http://www.thebowencenter.org/pages/theory.html

Casey, A. (2005). *Strengthening families/strengthening schools.* The Annie E. Casey Foundation. Retrieved on June 6, 2005, from http://www.aecf.org/initiatives/mc/sf/families/networks.htm.

Chao, R. & Good, G. (2004). Nontraditional students' perspectives on college education: A qualitative study. *Journal of College Counseling, 7,* 5-12.

Chartrand, J. (1992). An empirical test of a model of nontraditional student adjustment. *Journal of Counseling Psychology.* 39 (2), 193-202.

Clinton, H. (n.d.). *Higher education.* Retrieved on January 30, 2006, from http://clinton.senate.gov/issues/education/index.cfm?topic=higher

Craig, C. (1997). *Empowering nontraditional students.* Retrieved on November 27, 2005, from http://www.umkc.edu/cad/nade/nadedocs/97.html.

Creswell, J. (1998). *Qualitative inquiry and research design: Choosing among five traditions.* Thousand Oaks, CA: SAGE Publications, Inc.

Creswell, J. (2005). *Educational research: Planning, conducting, and evaluating quantitative and qualitative research.* Columbus, OH: Pearson Merrill Prentice Hall.

Donaldson, J. (1999). A model of college outcomes for adults. *Adult Education Quarterly. 50 (1)*, 24, 17. Retrieved on December 30, 2005, from file://E:\NontraditionalLearnerArticles\EBSCOhost.htm

Drawing conclusions and implications. (2005). Retrieved on December 30, 2005, from Graduate School of Education, George Mason University Web site: http://www.gse.gmu.edu/research/tr/TRconclusions.shtml

Dubois, J. (1989). *Factors related to participation and persistence of students enrolled in a Columbus, Ohio, Adult Basic Education program and the relationship of those factors to the adult students perceptions of their participation in post-secondary education.* Ohio: Ohio State University.

Deffand, Marie de Vichy Chamrond, marquise Du. *Letters of the Marquise du Deffand to the Hon. Horace Walpole.* Ed. Mary Berry. 4 vols. London: Longman, Hurst, Rees, and Orme, 1810.

Eldridge, D. (1994). Developing coherent community support networks. *Family Matters, (37)*, 56-59. Retrieved on June 8, 2005, from http://www.aifs.gov.au/institute/pubs/fm1/fm37de.html.

Eppler, M., Carsen-Plentl, C. & Harju, B. (2000). Achievement goals, failure attributions, and academic performance in nontraditional and traditional college students. *Journal of Social Behavior and Personality.* 15(3), 353-372.

Field, J. (2005). Social capital and lifelong learning. *The Encyclopedia of Informal Education.* Retrieved on June 10, 2005, from http://www.infed.org/lifelonglearning/social_capital_and_lifelong_learning.html.

FIF (n.d.) *What is a personal network?* Retrieved on October 25, 2008 from http://www.fifnc.org/connections/personal_networks.html

Fram, E. & Bonvillian, G. (2002). *Employees as part-time students: Is stress threatening the quality of their business education?* Retrieved on December 9, 2005, from http://www.questia.com/PM.qst?action=print&docId=5001040017

Glossary of mixed methods terms/concepts. (2003). Retrieved on January 30, 2006, from Florida International University Web site: http://ultraseek.fiu.edu/query.html?qt-glossary&qc=fiu+fiulib &col=fiu+fiulib

Greer, L. (1998). *Student support services and success factors for adult online learners.* Retrieved on September 11, 2005, from http://horizon.unc.edu/ts/editor/58.html

Groben, K., (1997). Stressed-out students find different modes of support. *The digital Collegian.* Retrieved on June 6, 2005, from http://www.collegian.psu.edu/archive/1997/12/12-15-97m01-014.asp.

Carey, K., Hess, F., Kelly, A., and Schneider, M. (2009) *Diplomas and dropouts.* Which colleges actually graduate their students and which don't? Washington, DC: American Enterprise Institute.

Heylighten, J. (1992) *What is systems theory?* Retrieved on November 3, 2008 from http://pespmc1.vub.ac.be/SYSTHEOR.html

Jone Johnson Lewis. *Bernice Johnson Reagon Quotes.* About Women's History. Retrieved on January 4, 2010 from: http://womenshistory.about.com/od/quotes/a/reagon_quotes.htm

Kempner, K., & Kinnick, M. (1990). Catching the window of opportunity: Being on time for higher education. *Journal of Higher Education,* 61(5), p. 535.

Kerka, S. (1995). *Adult learner retention revisited.* (Report No. 166). Columbus, OH: ERIC Clearinghouse on Adult Career and Vocational Education. (ERIC Document Reproduction Service No. ED389880.

Kirschner, P. & Van Bruggen, J. (2004). Learning and understanding in virtual teams. *CyberPsychology & Behavior*, 7, (2). Retrieved on June 6, 2005, from http://www.liebertonline.com

Kostere, K. (2005). *Qualitative analysis II: Qualitative research models and data analysis.* Retrieved on April 9, 2006 from Capella University Web site: https://www.capella.edu/Portal/Learner/SContent/colloquia2/sessions/oct04/docs2/Handout_-_Research_-_Qualitative_Analysis_in_Psychology_Part_II.doc

Leonard, M. (2002). *An outreach framework for retaining nontraditional students at open-admissions institutions.* Retrieved on December 9, 2005, from http://www.questia.com/PM.qst?action=print&docId=5000811198

Lincoln, Y. & Guba, E. (1985). *Naturalistic inquiry.* Newbury Park, CA: Sage Publications, Inc.

Lundberg, C. (2004). The influence of time-limitations, faculty, and peer relationships on adult student learning: a causal model. *Journal of Higher Education.* 74(6). 655+.

Moen, P. & Sweet, S. (2004). From 'work-family' to 'flexible careers' a life course reframing. *Community, Work & Family.* 7(2). 209-226.

Muench, K. (1987, October) *A comparative study of the psychosocial needs of adult men and women students in an adult degree program.* Paper presented at the annual meeting of the American Association for Adult and Continuing Education, Washington, DC.

Oehlkers, R. (1998). Focus – informal support. *Distance Education Systemwide Interactive Electronic Newsletter,* 3.9. Retrieved on September 16, 2005, from http://www.uwex.edu/disted/desien/1998/9809/focus.htm

Olson, D. (2000). Circumplex model of marital and family systems. *Journal of Family Therapy.* (22)2. 144-146.

Patton, M.Q. (1990). *Qualitative evaluation and research methods* (2nd ed.). Newbury Park, CA: Sage.

Project Guidance Online for those Learning at a Distance (GOLD). (n.d.). *Research methods glossary. Index of terms.* Retrieved on January 30, 2006, from http://www.bath.ac.uk/e-learning/gold/glossary.html

Pilisuk, M., Montgomery, M., Parks, S. & Acredolo, C. (2002). *Locus of control, life stress, and social networks: gender differences in the health status of the elderly.* Retrieved on January 14, 2006, from http://www.questia.com/PM.qst?action=print&docId=5001668398

Pugliesi, K. & Shook, S. (2002). *Gender, ethnicity, and network characteristics: variation in social support resources.* Retrieved on January 14, 2006, from http://www.questia.com/PM.qst?action=print&docId=5001335242

Rendón, L. (1998). *Helping nontraditional students be successful in college.* Retrieved on January 30, 2006, from http://www.natpoly.edu/library/reserve/6039.html

Richardson, J. & King, E. (2002). *Adult students in higher education: burden or boon?* Retrieved on November 27, 2005 from, http://www.questia.com/PM.qst?action=print&docId=5001332206

Rourke, L. (2000). *Operationalizing social interaction in computer conferencing.* Retrieved on March 10, 2006, from http://www.ulaval.ca/aced2000cade/francais/Actes/Rourke-Liam.html

Schopler, J. & Galinsky, M. (2002). *Support groups as open systems: a model for practice and research.* Retrieved on January 14, 2006, from http://questia.com/PM.qst?action=print&docId=5000221748

Schuller, T., Preston, J., Hammond, C., Brassett-Grundy, A. & Bynner, J. (2004). *The benefits of learning.* Retrieved on

January 14, 2006, from http://www.questia.com/PM.qst?actio n=print&docId=108400864

Sciba, M. (n.d.). *A study identifying the obstacles that nontraditional students face at Saginaw Valley State University.* Retrieved on September 16, 2005, from http://www.svsu.edu/writingprogram/braun02/study.htm

Seibert, A. & Karr, M. (2003) *The adult student's guide to survival & success.* Portland, OR: Practical Psychology Press.

Seepersad, S. (2002). *Family theory and systems theory.* Retrieved on January 14, 2006, from http://www.webofloneliness.com/publications/critical/systems_theory.htm

Semple, S. Howieson, C. & Paris, M. (2002). *Young people's transitions: careers support from family and friends.* Retrieved on January 14, 2006, from http://www.guidance-research.org/EG/impprac/imprguidconpol/scot/pracscot/careerdevelopment/suppfamilyand friends

Simcox, M. (1998). *The phenomenon of persistence in nontraditional graduates of hospital-based nursing schools: a phenomenologic study.* Retrieved on September 16, 2005, from http://www2.widener.edu/egr0001/dissertations/Simcox.html

Taniguchi, H. & Kaufman, G. (2005). Degree completion among nontraditional college students. *Social Science Quarterly.* 86(4).

The Chronicle of Higher Education. (1999). *99-00 Almanac.* Retrieved on November 20, 2005, from http://chronicle.com/free/almanac/1999/nation/nation.htm

Thompson, C., Jahn, E., Kopelman, R. & Prottas, D. (2005). *Perceived organizational family support: a longitudinal and multilevel analysis.* Retrieved on January 14, 2006, from http://www.questia.com/PM.qst?action=print&docId=50087 54278

Timarong, A., Temaungil, M. & Sukrad, W. (n.d.). Adult learning and learners. *Pacific Resources for Education and Learning.* Retrieved on September 11, 2005, from http://prel.org/products/pr_/adult-learners.htm

Timmons, J., Moloney, M., Dreilinger, D. & Schuster, J. (2002). Making dreams a reality: Using personal networks to achieve goals as you prepare to leave high school. *Tools for inclusion. 10*, (2). Retrieved on June 6, 2005, from Institute for Community Inclusion database.

UCLA WRC (n.d.). Returning to school – going back to go forward. *Returning student handbook.* Retrieved on September 11, 2005, from http://www.thecenter.ucla.edu/return.html

U.S. Department of Education, National Center for Education Statistics, (1998). *Choosing a postsecondary institution.* NCES 98-080, by C. Dennis Carroll. Washington, DC: Office of Educational Research and Improvement.

U.S. Department of Education, National Center for Education Statistics, (2000). *The condition of education 2000, Glossary.* NCES 2003-067, Washington, DC: U.S. Government Printing Office.

U.S. Department of Education, National Center for Education Statistics, (2002). *Nontraditional Undergraduates,* NCES 2002-012, by Susan Choy. Washington, DC: Office of Educational Research and Improvement.

U.S. Department of Education, National Center for Education Statistics, (2003). Appendix D. Glossary. *Projections of Education Statistics to 2013.* Retrieved September 24, 2005, from http://nces.ed.gov/programs/projections/appendix_D.asp

VanManen, M. (2000) *Phenomenology online: glossary.* Retrieved on April 9, 2006 from http://www.phenomenologyonline.com/glossary/glossary.html

Wegerif, R. (1998). The social dimension of asynchronous learning networks. *Journal of Asynchronous Learning Networks.* (2)1. p.16.

Wilson, T. (2002). *Returning to college is a family affair.* Retrieved on September 11, 2005, from http://selfgrowth.com

Author Index

Acredolo, C., 15, 19, 34, 90

Bauer, D., 34, 85
Bauman, S., 3, 4, 12, 85
Bell, J., 31, 85
Benshoff, J., 25, 30, 86
Bird, J., 3, 22-23, 86
Bonvillian, G., 31, 88
Bowen, M., 20, 86
Brassett-Grundy, A., 24, 90
Bynner, J., 24, 90

Carsen-Plentl, C., 35, 87
Casey, A., 38, 86
Chao, R., 25, 86

Chartrand, J., 34, 86
Clinton, H., 9, 36, 86
Craig, C., 1, 86
Creswell, J., xiv, 9, 39, 41, 86

DeLeon, C., 3, 12, 85
Donaldson, J., 30, 87
Dreilinger, D., 26, 29, 92
Dubois, J., 27, 87
Du Deffand, M., 78, 87

Field, J., 28, 33, 87
FIF, 15, 87
Fram, E., 31, 88

Galinsky, M., 23-24, 90

Good, G., 25, 86

Greer, L., 23, 88

Groben, K., 27, 88

Hammond, C., 24, 90

Harju, B., 35, 87

Heylighten, J. 16, 88

Howieson, C., 16, 88

Jahn, E., 19, 91

Kafentzis, J., 3, 12, 85

Karr, M., 27, 91

Kaufman, G., 33, 91

Kerka, S., 28, 88

King, E., 2, 3, 22, 90

Kinnick, M., 35, 88

Kirschner, P., 28, 89

Kopelman, R., 19, 91

Leonard, M., 8, 89

Lewis, L., 25, 30, 86

Lindsey, M., 3, 12, 85

Lundberg, C., 31-32, 89

Moen, P., 18-19, 89

Moloney, M., 26, 29, 92

Montgomery, M., 15, 19, 34, 90

Morgan, C., 3, 22-23, 86

Mott, D., 34, 85

Muench, K., 30, 89

Oehlkers, R., 23, 89

Olson, D., vii, 21, 89

Paris, M., 31, 91

Parks, S., 15, 19, 34, 90

Patton, M., 39, 90

Pilisuk, M., 15, 19, 34-35, 90

Preston, J., 24, 90

Prottas, D., 19, 91

Pugliesi, K., 19, 90

Reagon, B., 1, 88

Rendón, L., 26, 30, 31, 90

Richardson, J., 2, 3, 22, 90

Rourke, L., 28, 90

Schopler, J., 23-24, 90

Schuller, T., 24, 90

Schuster, J., 26, 29, 92

Sciba, M., 29-30, 91

Seepersad, S., 21, 91

Seibert, A., 27, 91

Semple, S., 31, 91

Shook, S., 19, 90

Simcox, M., 27, 91

Sukrad, W., 27, 92

Sweet, S., 18-19, 89

Taniguchi, H., 33, 91

Temaungil, M., 27, 92

Thompson, C., 19, 91

Timarong, A., 27, 92

Timmons, J., 26, 29, 92

VanBruggen, J., 28, 89

VanManen, M. 13, 16, 92

Wang, N., 6, 3, 12, 85

Wegerif, R., 28, 93

Wilson, T., 37-38, 93

Zavala-Lopez, M., 3, 12, 85